A WORLD OF HEARTY SOUPS

A WORLD OF HEARTY SOUPS

John Philips Cranwell

AVENEL BOOKS • NEW YORK

FOR BRENDA,

Who has taught me more about cooking than I am willing to admit, even to myself

0-517-020912

Library Of Congress Catalog Card Number: 68-31893

This edition is published by Avenel Books
a division of Crown Publishers, Inc.
by arrangement with Funk & Wagnalls
a b c d e f g h
Manufactured in the United States Of America

PREFACE

A NUMBER of years ago I thought that writing a preface to a book was rather difficult. I now know that this is an illusion. After all, when you come to write the preface, the manuscript is finished and all the writer has to do is to thank the people who helped him.

No book, not even a work of fiction, is the product of one man, be he ever so erudite and imaginative. The writer gets varying degrees of assistance. Even if he be married to a shrew—which I hasten to say I am not, although the metaphor is apt in a cookbook as a shrew eats three times its own weight in a day—her very shrewishness is a spur. It compels him, the author, to retire to his study, den, garret, office, or wherever he works just to avoid her. Because he wants to avoid her he works longer hours than most writers. In one of his essays, H. L. Mencken said something to the effect that any writer who says he writes eight hours a day is a liar, if he writes for four he is working hard.

Nonfiction writers usually have a long list of people to thank. Some are laborers in libraries or in love. Others are researchers, friends, sources of inspiration; and there are people—professional proofreaders, and others—whose aid has been instrumental, nay, invaluable in the preparation of the book.

Cookbook authors have special problems in this field. Friends and relations provide "guidance"—"without the faith in me of my dear Aunt Agnes [the writer probably poisoned her for her money] I should never have been able to complete this tome." People who write that way always refer to books as tomes, or sometimes, volumes. Or perhaps the acknowledgment goes like this: "Had I not had the affection of my dear young cousin, Susy Q, who learned many things at my knee, including how to scramble eggs, I should never have had the courage to undertake this work, let alone complete it." One wonders to what heights, culinary of course, Susy reached for her scrambled eggs.

Seriously, however, a writer of cookbooks has to thank many more people than do writers of other kinds of books. In addition to the inspirational types he must include in his acknowledgments other categories of people. There are those whose trust was so great that they tasted his experiments despite their ulcers. Some provided old and treasured recipes. Another group, usually better cooks than the author, were helpful with culinary suggestions about things he had never cooked before. (Here I think of a calf's head.) And, finally, the author of a cookbook is obligated to the writers of other cookbooks from which he has pillaged, purloined, or plagiarized recipes, being careful always, of course, to make small changes which render him legally unassailable. This last group of unwitting assistants usually remain anonymous. They will so remain here.

My list is a short one. Most of the people I have to thank contributed in more than one way. And for that reason I shall not be too specific in my acknowledgments. I should add that all of them tasted one recipe or another and—I am happy to say—suffered no ill effects.

I were ingrate indeed not to mention with thanks the extraordinary contributions of my old friend Peterkin Pepit, world traveler, gourmet, tosspot, and conversationalist. In the same breath—or sentence—must I thank, too, our mutual friend, Dr. F. X. Dottle, the great orthopedist and gastronome. Both gentlemen were sources of inspiration, suggestion—many unsuitable for a family cookbook—and unusual recipes.

My dear friends Gregory and Mary Hutchison, who are much better cooks than I, not only tasted, made suggestions, and gave demonstrations, but also saved me from the inclusion of a Japanese recipe which would have been worse than a crime. It would have been a fault. In addition to the Hutchisons, others who tasted and suggested were Shirley Mecklin, Darcy Albertson, Rosemary McDermott, Marian Priest, and Isabelle Carpenter, who also contributed no little in the typing department.

I want to thank, as well, Barbara Kean for instructions on bread baking and also for her willingness to experiment in the matter of tasting. I owe a special debt to another friend and neighbor, Hazel Detwiler, for much sampling, many suggestions, and the recipe as well as the ingredients for a unique soup made from ferns. Another entitled to my gratitude is Lee Perkins, who, as though a follower of Henry V, entered the breach at a critical time and helped with the final editing, thus enabling the book to meet the publisher's deadline, a necessary but abhorrent thing to writers.

Lastly, but not leastly—a splendid phrase—I am pleased to include in this list of creditors my wife; she not only tasted many of my soups and suggested important changes in recipes, but also put up with me during the writing of this book, no small thing. The wife of a writer never gets enough credit for her husband's work, *ita uti supra demonstravimus*. Everything I have written has been the better for her counsel.

J. P. C.

Washington
April, 1968

CONTENTS

I

HEARTY SOUPS MAKE THE MEAL

WE HAVE it on excellent authority that man cannot live on bread alone, but with a good soup added to the menu he can do very well. A cognate authority mentions bread—in another connection—as the staff of life. Perhaps soup is the distaff. In any case, between the two they make a complete meal; add salad, you have a feast; include wine, and you have a fiesta. It were bootless to extol the merits of soup. The fond theory that fifty million people of any nationality cannot be wrong is, on the face of it, absurd, but when the hardy peasantry of all the world has subsisted for centuries on little more than soup and bread, the conclusion is obvious: soup has merit. Indeed, most of the world's hearty gourmet soups have had lowly beginnings. French Onion Soup, Bouillabaisse, the various Bean Soups, Borshch, Lentil Soup, Brunswick Stew, the list is endless. Some we eat now with little or no change from the original recipes handed down in families as cherished possessions. Others have been refined over the years by the addition of wine or seasoning, or by changed methods of cooking, until they are today among the elite dishes of gastronomy. And, except in the United States alas, bread has sprung from the same roots and marched with the soups.

So much for irrefutable generalizations. If they do not create an irresistible urge to hie yourself to the kitchen and get out the soup kettle, I am a poor pleader—in the legal sense—or you do not enjoy cooking. Or, perhaps, you lack a soup kettle. Buy one. It is probably the greatest culinary invention since Prometheus stole fire from heaven—a grievous crime and grievously he paid for it, but everyone everywhere owes him a great debt. There are thousands of fine dishes in the world because of that theft. But for day-in and day-out eating, come rain or shine, sleet, gloom of night, hail or snow, fair or foul, torrid or freezing, give me soup.

After the preceding flights of fancy and purple prose, the prosaic fact is that this recipe book was born of too much leisure, coupled with inordinate laziness. For a long time most of my lunches and many of my suppers, particularly those following that vicious and insidious gathering known as a cocktail party, have consisted of a good soup, a loaf of bread, and a jug of wine. The bough was omitted as I am an inveterate anti-picnicker. Nor do I like "cook-outs," a vile term in any case. It was not long before I grew tired of Vegetable Soup, Cream of Tomato, and the like, and began looking around—unweepingly I might add—for more soups to conquer. I found them, of course, from various parts of the world. Some in such imaginary compendia as *One Thousand and One Ways to Cook with Retsina, How To Laye Down a Goode Soupe With a Prity Maide,* and *The Art of Missionary Cookery.* That is a charming old volume written in the Congo almost fifty years ago. The marinades are especially interesting although occasionally grisly.

In any case I gradually collected a number of excellent recipes for soups that were hearty, nourishing, and a pleasure to eat. One cannot always go leafing through a library of cookbooks, particularly those unindexed, looking for a recipe, so I began writing down on cards the recipes, with the changes I had wrought for my own taste. My filing system being what it is, of course, I could never find anything I wanted when I wanted it. So what to do? To do was to put them all down in a book. Then I could lose them all at once or find them all in the same place.

When finally—after a week of searching—I got all my cards together, I found that I had recipes from every area of the world. I selected those that I thought were the best for the main course at a lunch or supper. They, with a few others to be mentioned later, make up this book.

Another group of soups had perforce to be omitted. Although they clearly make excellent one-dish meals, the ingredients, fresh, dried, or canned, are not available in the United States. Most of these originate in the western Pacific area. One famous soup thus deleted is from Australia. It is made from kangaroo tails. To a degree the same flaw occurs in Japanese and Polynesian soups. Some Oriental grocery stores in the larger cities carry canned and dried foods from Japan, but soup made from them lacks the charm of soups made from fresh ingredients. So, at least, I am told by friends and gourmets who have lived where once the Shogun ruled. Curiously and inexplicably the same is not true of imported Chinese ingredients. As a result most of the soups from the Far East included herein are from the Flowery Kingdom. While in a number of instances I have used substitutes, always noted as such in the recipe, because the actual materials are not imported, the substitute is a very close approximation of the original and the resulting soup suffers little in taste or texture.

Originally I had planned to use only those recipes which described how to make soups in the traditional manner. A few could be cooked in forty minutes, a few others could be prepared in an hour, but the great majority required from two hours to two or three days. Fortunately my wife, who has a very practical mind and a very forthright tongue—what better critic can you have?—read some fifty recipes. Her comment: "For you these recipes are fine. You don't mind slaving over a hot stove for two days to make the dish you want. Some of our friends are equally happy at the prospect. But what you are trying to sell is hard work. You're out of your mind." As usual, I took her advice.

As a result, most of the recipes are divided into two parts, marked "I" and "II."

All recipes marked "I" can be made in an hour or less. A number of other soups have only one recipe. Most of these can be made from raw materials in about an hour. A few other soups with only one version require considerably more than an hour to make but are so outstanding that to omit them from this book would be a culinary error. The ingredients of these soups are so integrated with each other in the cooking that short cuts are impossible. Among these magnificent dishes are two Chinese soups and the products of Creole cookery, notably the gumbos. Failure to include soups from New Orleans would be an act almost as unpatriotic as that of the man without a country. Creole cookery, taken as a whole, is the only cuisine indigenous to the United States which can be considered a contribution to gastronomy. This is not to say that individual American dishes are not among the world's most succulent. It is to say, however, that the cuisine developed in and about New Orleans is unique.

It should be noted here that, while most of the long versions of the soups are more satisfying than their shorter counterparts, the latter provide exceedingly good fare. Indeed, a few of the quick recipes give results as good as, and in at least one instance better than, the slower versions.

Any technical manual, and a cookbook or recipe book is a technical manual, must define certain terms if it is to be intelligible to its readers. Most of these definitions will be found in the Glossary. As well as being a glossary, it is a how-to-do-it section. There such terms as "bouquet garni," "roux," and "velouté sauce," among others, are defined and their preparation detailed. The Appendix contains a short list of the utensils essential to making the soups in this book. Certain general terms, however, should be cleared up here.

First is the matter of "seafood" and "fish." The words are not interchangeable. Theoretically "seafood" would appear to apply to all the denizens of the vasty deep, but for the purposes of this book, and by common usage, it refers to shrimp, lobster, oysters, clams, octopus, crayfish, mussels, to name a few, but not to fish. "Fish" covers all finny creatures from the waters, including mammals such as whales and porpoises—although neither appears in the recipes. If the recipes seem to be weighted in favor of seafood, it is because I enjoy it. Like Grendel's mother, I was brought up near the water—the Chesapeake Bay. As a sometime writer on naval matters I have a double incentive to look to the sea as a source of sustenance.

Germane to the preceding paragraph is the matter of "chowders." According to the Merriam-Webster *International Dictionary*—second edition, naturally—the word "chowder" derives from the French word *chaudière*, a kind of large kettle or caldron. When French fishermen, particularly Bretons, returned successfully to their villages it was their custom to contribute part of their catch to a kind of communal dinner party. In certain parts of the United States it would have been called a "fish fry." The fishermen or their wives, however, did not fry the fish and seafood but put them into a *chaudière*, along with vegetables, herbs, and perhaps a bit of meat or poultry. In view of the French culinary *mystique* one can be reasonably sure that village vied with village to produce the best possible *chaudière*. In any case, when French fishermen came to the new world they brought their customs and caldrons with them. Eventually *chaudière* was anglicized as "chowder."

From this bit of culinary history it is evident that a chowder is a dish based on seafood and fish. All other ingredients are incidental. To call a dish made of potatoes, corn, or vegetables a chowder is patently a misnomer. All the chowders described in this book, therefore, are based on products of the ocean, or an occasional river.

The word "stew" calls not so much for definition as for differentiation. Webster gives a number of choices. "Stew" means a dish made of meat, vegetables, and some kind of liquid; it is served hot, but, and this is the operative point, it is eaten with a *fork*. "Stew" also means a brothel—but back to the stove. Further, and this is the important definition, oysters are stewed—as are some people from time to time—but oyster stew is *not* eaten with a fork. As the first two definitions are clearly beyond the compass of a book about soup, stews in these recipes will be made on the principle of the third definition.

Similar in many respects, but vastly different in others, is a gumbo. Gumbos are in a class by themselves, and what a class it is! They are all grouped together in the section on Creole cookery. So now are these three: chowders, stews, and gumbos, and the greatest of these . . . wéll, *de gustibus non est disputandum*.

So much for general definitions. A few other items pertaining to this book should be mentioned. One of these is the use of brand names in the recipes. When they appear, it is for one of two reasons. Either it is the only product of its kind that I know, or it is a product with many competitors but the one with which I am familiar. In the first instance, the brand name may help your local merchant find it for you if he does not stock it. In the second instance, if you prefer brand X, by all means use it; it is probably just as good as the one mentioned. Be guided here by that old adage "Stick to the devil you know."

In calculating the time required to prepare the following recipes, or at least the shorter versions, I have presumed that the basic stock—see below—is at hand. Most stocks can be made well ahead of time and refrigerated over several days until needed. When the stock is produced as an integral part of cooking the other ingredients, the time necessary for this process is included in the overall estimate.

Several old saws tell us that you cannot make something without something else; e.g., you cannot make bricks without straw. I suspect this statement is outmoded long since but it serves still as an adage. Another is that you cannot make omelets without breaking eggs. I doubt that proper omelets can ever be made any other way. Much the same thing applies to soup. You cannot make soup, or much of it, without some kind of bouillon, broth, or in the case of fish and seafood soups, a fumet. For the sake of simplicity and consistency these will all be referred to in the recipes as "stock," with the descriptive words "beef," "chicken," "fish," or other identifier preceding each. Because of the importance of stock as an ingredient the first three recipes in the book deal with it. They are beef stock, chicken stock, and fish stock or fumet.

For those who are primarily interested in the "quick" part of this book and cannot spare the time to make the basic stocks, another method is readily available. This method is known as "purchasing." There are several varieties of concentrated beef stock on the market. Commercially prepared "beef broths" are excellent substitutes for that made in your own kitchen. Chicken stock can be provided in the same way or by the use of an instant "chicken broth mix," a dry extract which comes in jars. I prefer the latter to canned chicken broth because it contains less fat. Finally, a substitute for fish stock—or fumet—is clam juice. This substitute, while acceptable, will slightly alter the flavor of the soup in which it is used. If these substitutes are employed, omit salt and pepper from the recipe you are using until after you have tasted the final dish. Commercial products usually contain considerable seasoning.

For those cooks who wish to try making the basic stocks in their own kitchens, the following recipes are included.

BEEF STOCK

(2 *quarts*)

1 leek
1 small onion
3 cloves
1 stalk celery with leaves
1 carrot
1½ pounds lean stewing beef
1 pound beef bones
1 bay leaf
2 teaspoons salt

Wash leek and cut into three pieces. Peel onion and stick in the cloves. Break celery in half. Scrape carrot and cut into thirds. Chop meat into large cubes. Place all ingredients in a large, heavy saucepan. Add three quarts water. Cover, and bring to a boil. Remove from heat and skim off any scum that may have arisen. Return to low heat and simmer slowly for five hours. Remove from fire. Skim off fat and strain the contents of the pot through a fine sieve or chinoise. Discard solid contents of sieve.

CHICKEN STOCK
(2 *quarts*)

To make chicken stock the same ingredients and method are used, *ita uti supra demonstravimus,* except for beef and beef bones. For these, substitute two and a half pounds chicken backs and wings.

FISH STOCK (Fumet)
(2 *quarts*)

1 yellow onion, about 4 ounces
butter
12 parsley sprigs
2 pounds fish bones and trimmings
juice of one lemon
1 cup dry white wine

Peel and slice onion. Half fill a large saucepan with water. Add onion. Bring water to a boil and simmer about ten minutes to blanch. Meanwhile, lightly grease the bottom of a large saucepan with butter. Drain onions and place them in the saucepan. Add parsley and on top of that, put the fish bones and trimmings. Add the lemon juice. Cover the saucepan and cook over a very low flame for about five minutes. Shake the pan from time to time. Remove cover. Add the white wine and allow to boil gently until the liquid has been reduced by half. Add four quarts water and bring to a boil. Skim and cook uncovered for twenty minutes over a moderate flame. Strain, reserving the stock and discarding everything else.

PUBLISHER'S NOTE

Some terms used in the list of ingredients for a recipe or in the cooking directions are followed by a (G). An explanation of that term or, in some cases, a recipe for its preparation will be found in the Glossary which is arranged alphabetically. The Glossary begins on page 179.

II

NORTH AMERICA

HABITANT PEA SOUP

(*Serves 4*)

One of my earliest experiences with "foreign" food was on a trip to Canada. I found little in the city of Quebec of great gastronomic interest (in Montreal it was an entirely different kettle of fish) but some of the small roadside restaurants between the American border and Quebec provided what could be described as simple but excellent fare. One of the dishes for which this part of Canada is justly famous is Habitant Pea Soup. The inclusion of this recipe serves two purposes. It provides an excellent meal and is exactly the right soup to combine with Cream of Tomato to make Potage Mongole (page 117). For whichever reason you make the soup, you will be rewarded for your trouble. If you use split peas which must be soaked overnight and then cooked three hours, this dish will require a great deal longer than is really necessary. There are excellent yellow split peas available which need not be soaked and which can be reduced to the proper state of mushiness in about forty-five minutes. The use of a blender will permit the soup to be made in about one hour.

1 pound split peas
3 large onions
2 carrots
6 celery tops
6 large sprigs parsley
4 bay leaves
1 pound Canadian bacon
¼ teaspoon cayenne pepper
salt
pepper
small croutons (G)

Put two and one half quarts water in a large soup kettle, add split peas, cover, and bring to a simmer. While water is reaching the proper temperature, peel onions, scrape carrots, and chop both, not too small. Add to kettle. Chop celery tops and parsley. Add celery, parsley, and bay leaves and continue to simmer, covered, until peas are mushy, about forty-five minutes. Meanwhile, fry the bacon until crisp and drain on paper towels. Chop into small squares and add to the kettle when the peas are cooked. Put in the cayenne pepper, stir well, taste, add salt and pepper as needed. Serve very hot with a bowl of croutons provided for each diner.

SUGGESTED MENU

No bread is necessary. A sliced cucumber and lettuce salad garnished with a few strips of pimento dressed in the French manner should be served after the soup. The wine should be *vin ordinaire,* preferably red. It is the best accompaniment in this department.

SCALLOP CHOWDER MURRAY BAY

(*Serves* 4)

The most delicate of seafoods used in chowders are probably scallops. Of scallops the most delicate are bay scallops, as opposed to deep-sea scallops. The latter measure about an inch and a half to a side, while bay scallops—it matters not what bay they come from—are little bigger than the end of a small man's thumb. My first experience with the bay variety was on a freighter which ran from Montreal along the south shore of the Saint Lawrence and out to the Magdalen Islands, but which, alas, runs no more. (Damn airplanes and trucks!) The food aboard was remarkably good, and sometimes rather strange, including cod tongues for example. Occasionally the martini-infused traveler was offered bay scallops. Even lapped in a flour-egg mixture and fried in deep fat, they were delicious—better even than the ordinary variety cooked with the most delicate of sauces. Both kinds may be used in making chowder. Onions, a normal ingredient of chowders, should be avoided in this instance; they overpower the taste of the scallops. Leeks make a fine substitute. For some reason, not immediately apparent, scallop chowder seldom appears on restaurant menus, and recipes for it are scarce. Hence this original one.

If you work hard at it, you can do this soup in about an hour. A shorter version could be contrived but the time saved would be negligible, and the soup not so good. Start a little earlier; the effort will not be wasted.

4 slices bacon
3 medium leeks
3 stalks celery
2 medium potatoes
1½ pounds scallops
5 tablespoons butter
2 tablespoons flour
1 quart milk
½ tablespoon salt
1 teaspoon freshly ground black pepper
1 pimento

Crisp the bacon in a skillet, discard bacon fat and chop the bacon, not too small. While bacon is cooking, wash leeks, and slice them into thin rounds, using about half the green tops. Chop the celery small; peel and dice the potatoes. If the scallops are deep-sea scallops, cut them to the size of bay scallops. Put three tablespoons butter in a large saucepan. Melt over a low flame and cook the leeks and celery until soft, but do not allow to brown. Add the potatoes and one pint of milk. Cook over a low fire until potatoes are tender (this will take about half an hour) but do not allow liquid to simmer. While the potatoes are cooking, place the remaining butter in another saucepan, melt, add the flour and make a roux(G). When the roux is cooked, about five minutes, gradually add the remaining milk to make a thin sauce. Put the salt and pepper in the saucepan with the potatoes, stir well and continue to cook. Cut the pimento fine. When the potatoes are tender, add the thin sauce to the other saucepan. Put in the scallops, bacon, and pimento. Cover and allow to cook very slowly without simmering until the scallops are done, ten or fifteen minutes. Serve very hot in soup plates. If the chowder is too thick, thin it with a little milk.

SUGGESTED MENU

Despite the delicacy of the scallops, this chowder is a fairly heavy dish and should be followed by a light salad. With potatoes an inherent element, no bread is required, but you might serve saltines or some other form of cracker on the side. A light white table wine from California or the Rhine would complement the soup very well.

CANUCK DUCK SOUP RIVIÈRE DE RENARD

(*Serves* 6)

A number of years ago, while making an excursion down the Saint Lawrence on a freighter, a close friend, Dr. F. Xenophon Dottle discovered a method of making duck soup. After some effort, Dr. Dottle and our mutual friend and coadjutor, Peterkin Pepit, succeeded in deciphering the recipe, despite the fact that the original document seemed to have been immersed for some time in a sunken fishing vessel just off the mouth of the Fox River. Apparently it was written in indelible ink on a piece of shark's skin. When translated, it read as follows:

"Just the place for a lark," the hunter cried,
  As he leveled his piece with care.
The lark escaped, but he got two ducks
  With a single shot in the air.
"Not the right size for a brace of duck pies,"
  He sighed all adroop,
"But by adding some rice and cider and spice
  We could have a most succulent soup . . .
"With bacon, of course." (He ate like a horse.)

Meanwhile at Fox River, his dame cooked calf's liver,
  And hoped for his early return.
Any silly delay, or a halt by the way, and
  Their breakfast was certain to burn.
The meat was quite sere—he stopped for a beer—
  And his wife was properly wroth.
But the sight of the fowl,
  Converted her howl to "They'll make an
Excellent broth . . .
  "Go fetch me an onion, some wine, and some sage,
Four sprigs of parsley, some herbs, and one bay;
  And while the soup's cooking we'll roll in the . . ."

At this point they were interrupted by the rowdy entrance of four wild-eyed men, one with a harp, another smoking an enormous cigar. Three of the new arrivals shouted in unison, as though their name were Stentor: "DUCK SOUP."

The original recipe obviously calls for two wild ducks. If they are unavailable, substitute one domestic duck. After all, as Peterkin Pepit always said, "You can help her become feral," which will live up to the letter of the recipe, if not to the taste.

The recipe which Dr. Dottle discovered in such an unusual way is not conducive to early abandonment of the kitchen. I have, with his permission, therefore, devised a shortened version (I). The good doctor's original version (II), only slightly altered to use domestic duck, will follow the quick version. The reader and, presumably, cook should be warned that if the quick version of Mock Dragon Soup is not the most expensive dish in this collection of recipes, the first version of Canuck Duck Soup is.

In any case, it is one of the richest soups listed. The recipe will feed six quite hungry people, and, in an emergency, could stretch to eight. But, once again, time is money, and if you lack the former, you will need the latter. Lacking either or both, make the soup the slow way. Dr. Dottle always thought the relaxed approach was better. Some people may find this version a little on the sweet side. There is not much you can do about it except, perhaps, replace sweet cider with hard. The substitution may send you reeling from the table. You have been warned. The quick method is:

I. Duck Soup de Renard (*Quick Version*)

(*Serves* 6)

bouquet garni (G)
  (1 small onion
  4 sprigs parsley
  1 bay leaf
  ½ teaspoon marjoram
  ½ teaspoon sage
  ¼ teaspoon mace)
1 pint sweet cider
1 quart good Burgundy
2 cans Reese's whole mallard duck
¾ cup sifted flour
2 cans cooked wild rice (15 oz. each)
1 teaspoon salt
½ teaspoon black pepper
1 generous jigger applejack

Make bouquet garni. Place cider and Burgundy in a saucepan, add bouquet garni, cover, and simmer gently twenty minutes. Meanwhile, remove ducks from cans, skim off duck fat and reserve. Drain ducks, reserving juice. Separate meat from bones, skin, and gristle. Cut up the meat into bite-size pieces. Place half a cup of the duck fat in a large, heavy saucepan; melt; add flour, to make a roux (G), cooking it over a slow fire for four minutes. Drain wild rice, and wash it under running tepid water for about one minute. When the twenty minutes are up, remove bouquet garni; gradually add the contents of the first saucepan to the second, and bring slowly to a boil, using a wire whisk to stir out any lumps. Put in reserved duck juice. If it is less than a quart, add water to bring it to that quantity. Put in duck meat, salt, pepper, applejack, and wild rice. Simmer very gently for five minutes, taste, correct seasoning if necessary, and soup is ready to serve. The finished soup should have the consistency of a light bisque. If it is too thick, thin with water. Do not allow the soup to cook, once the duck and wild rice have been added; merely heat thoroughly.

II. Duck Soup de Renard (*Traditional Version*)

(*Serves* 6)

1 cup raw wild rice
bouquet garni (G)
  (1 medium onion
  4 sprigs parsley
  1 bay leaf
  ½ teaspoon marjoram
  ½ teaspoon sage)
1 duck, cut up as for stewing
2 cups sweet cider
4 cups Burgundy
2 tablespoons arrowroot flour
salt
pepper
⅛ teaspoon mace
1½ ounces applejack

Wash the rice well in tepid water. Drain and place in a large soup kettle. Make bouquet garni. Put the duck on top of the rice, add the bouquet garni, and cover with the cider and Burgundy. Mix contents of the kettle well, bring to a boil, cover, and simmer two hours. Remove kettle from fire. Take out pieces of duck and place in a bowl to cool. Using a colander, strain liquid into another bowl and place in refrigerator to cool. Discard bouquet garni, and wash all fat from rice with tepid water. Return rice to kettle. When duck is cool enough to handle, remove and discard all bones, skin, and gristle. Cut the remaining meat into very small pieces. Put them on top of rice. Skim and discard (for the purposes of this soup only; it makes excellent shortening) all fat from top of liquid, and add liquid to the kettle. Pour in one quart water, cover, bring to a boil and simmer twenty-five minutes. No skimming is necessary. Meanwhile, mix the arrowroot flour with one half cup water to make a light smooth paste. Add to soup kettle, stir well, and simmer another five minutes. Taste, season with salt and pepper as required. Add mace and applejack, simmer another five minutes, and soup is ready for the table.

SUGGESTED MENU

An ideal bread with this soup is Maryland Beaten Biscuit (G)—there *are* wild ducks on the Chesapeake Bay—a baker's dozen to the customer. If you are going to make Beaten Biscuit, you might as well make thirty-six as six. It takes no longer. A very simple salad is best, for the soup is rich. The wine, of course, will be Burgundy.

G.I. BEAN SOUP

(*Serves 4*)

The letters "G.I." have come to mean the American soldier in what the British euphemistically call "other ranks." This is a normal etymological development. The initials actually stand for "Government Issue" and are applicable to anything the United States Government supplies to its employees and officials. This soup is produced by the United States Government and is served to members of Congress, who are Government officials. Hence it is properly G.I. Bean Soup. *Quod erat demonstrandum.* The Congress is divided in many ways, but the most important of these is its division into two branches: the Senate and the House of Representatives. Each has its own restaurant, and each restaurant always has bean soup on its menu. There is some disagreement on the events which led to the soup's continuous appearance on the Senate side. No such confusion exists on the side of the House.

Anyone who has spent a summer in Washington can understand why bean soup was omitted from the House restaurant luncheon menu on a hot, humid August day in 1904. The omission has never occurred since. Joseph G. (Uncle Joe) Cannon, the revered and autocratic Speaker of the House, went to the restaurant on that occasion especially to eat bean soup. Noting its absence, he is alleged to have exclaimed: "Thunderation! I had my mouth set for bean soup. From now on, hot or cold, rain, snow, or shine, I want it on the menu every day!" What Uncle Joe wanted in the House he usually got. It is still on the menu every day.

Bean soup recipes deriving from the Senate restaurant include mashed potatoes. This senatorial culinary *lèse majesté*, could not, of course, be perpetuated by any serious cookbook. The House restaurant version is very similar to that made by the recipe below.

Although not so good as the traditional version this quickie soup is a filling, delicious dish. It has the additional merit of speed. One can prepare it in less than thirty minutes, assuming, of course, one has the ingredients in the larder.

If you wish to eat the same soup that Uncle Joe Cannon was so fond of, regardless of the weather, you may do so by following recipe II.

I. G.I. Bean Soup (*Quick Version*)

(*Serves 4*)

2 medium onions
3 tablespoons butter
½ pound lean cooked ham slices (⅛ inch thick)
4 cans S. S. Pierce Old Fashioned Bean Soup (15½ oz.)

Peel the onions and chop small. Melt butter in a skillet and cook onions over a moderate flame until soft and golden. Do not allow to brown. While onions cook, cut ham into half-inch squares. Put soup in top half of double boiler. Add cooked onion and ham. Cover and heat over boiling water, stirring from time to time, until the soup is very hot. If the soup is too thick—and it may be for some tastes—thin with water.

II. G.I. Bean Soup (*Traditional Version*)

(*Serves* 4)

1½ pounds small navy beans
2 large onions
1 large clove garlic
2 tablespoons butter
bouquet garni (G)
  (4 sprigs parsley
  1 large bay leaf
  1 teaspoon thyme)
1½ pounds ham hocks with meat on them
3 teaspoons pepper
2 tablespoons arrowroot flour (optional)
salt

Soak the beans overnight, or for at least eight hours, with plenty of water to cover. Drain beans in colander. Run hot water over them for about ten minutes, or until they whiten. Chop onions coarsely, and mince garlic or put through a press. Pour three quarts water in a soup kettle, and bring to a boil. While water is heating, melt butter in a skillet and slowly cook the chopped onion and garlic, turning now and again, until both are slightly brown. Make bouquet garni. When water has come to a boil, add beans, onions and garlic, bouquet garni, ham hocks and pepper. Bring to a boil again, reduce heat, cover, and simmer for three hours. Remove from heat. Discard bouquet garni. Remove ham hocks, strip, and discard bones, skin, fat, and gristle. Chop lean meat into small pieces and reserve. Place one pint of the soup in a blender and blend for forty-five seconds at high speed. Return to kettle and stir well. This will help thicken the soup, which should be almost a purée but with ham pieces and whole beans in it. If a thicker soup is desired, place two tablespoons arrowroot flour in a small bowl, add six tablespoons of soup liquid and stir into a paste. Pour into soup kettle, add reserved ham, bring slowly to a boil, taste, and add salt as required. The salt must not be added until just before serving. Simmer for three minutes more to be sure soup is heated through. It is now ready.

SUGGESTED MENU

The traditional bread with this soup is hot corn sticks, accompanied by a plethora of butter. Hazel's Herbage (G) is light, a desirable characteristic in a dish following bean soup. Be one hundred percent American all the way and drink a good American mountain red wine from California.

VELOUTÉ DIEPPOISE

(*Serves 4*)

One of the few really great hotels in the United States is the Plaza in New York. Both Peterkin Pepit and Fergus Xenophon Dottle always stay there. In addition to the service one expects from such an establishment, it offers excellent food in its numerous restaurants. One of these is the Oak Room (restricted to men until three o'clock in the afternoon—the ladies have the Palm Court, of course. Incidental intelligence). While dining there with some men —unlike Sir Christopher Wren, I was not designing Saint Paul's— I had this remarkable soup. Normally, to say that an inn or restaurant serves "good hotel food" is to damn its cuisine, not with faint praise but with no praise at all. This dish is not in that category; it is good food anywhere.

Fortunately for all of us, the Plaza's executive chef, M. André René, was kind enough to share the recipe, which follows. To make the soup easier to prepare in kitchens lacking the culinary resources of a great hotel or restaurant, I have made a few minor changes, such as substituting oysters for mussels. I will not claim that the revision has improved the dish, but be sure to try it. It is a boon to the hurried cook as it takes less than an hour to prepare. If you like the soup as I make it, go to the Oak Room and taste what happens there.

2 quarts fish stock (p. 7)
1 pound raw shrimp
28 oysters
1 medium onion
2 stalks celery
1 large leek
8 tablespoons butter
1 clove garlic
1 small truffle
8 tablespoons flour
½ bottle dry white wine
½ cup light cream
salt
white pepper

Simmer shrimp in stock for about seven minutes. Remove shrimp, shell, and chop small. Reserve stock. Poach the oysters in their own liquor until oysters are plump, and edges curl (five to ten minutes).

While oysters poach, chop onion, celery, and leek into small pieces. When oysters are done, drain, reserving liquor and four oysters. Place butter in a large skillet and cook in it over a low flame the onion, celery, and leek. Add the garlic, either minced or put through a press. Cook until contents of skillet are soft but not brown. Meanwhile, mince the truffle. When vegetables are soft, add flour and make a roux (p. 191). While roux is cooking, bring fish stock to a simmer and gradually add one cup of the hot stock to the skillet, stirring to make a sauce. Stir sauce well into stock. Add truffle and remove from the fire. Put in the shrimp and the poached oysters. Add the wine. Place in a blender and blend at high speed for thirty seconds. Return to saucepan, add the cream. Stir well. Thin soup to desired consistency with the reserved oyster liquor. Taste, and correct seasoning with salt and pepper. Heat but do not boil. When ready to serve, garnish each plate with one of the reserved oysters.

SUGGESTED MENU

French bread or hard club rolls should accompany this soup. A salad made with fresh Belgian endive covered with a mustard dressing (G) should follow. Chablis always weds well with seafood and is most appropriate with Velouté Dieppoise.

CLAM CHOWDER MILES STANDISH

(Serves 4)

The widely held belief that Priscilla fed John this version of Massachusetts clam chowder to give him the courage to speak for himself has no historical foundation. With one or two plates of this delectable chowder inside him, John is more likely to have gone to sleep than to have made a proposal of marriage, seemingly the only kind of proposal that Priscilla was prepared to entertain. But the chowder speaks for itself. It makes a magnificent meal. And fresh clams are available the year round.

It is meet here to say a few words about the cooking of clams. The less bivalves are cooked the more tender they are. Hence one would conclude that raw clams are more tender than cooked clams, and one would be right. If clams are to be cooked in a liquid, they should be brought swiftly to a boil, removed immediately from the fire, and drained. Even then their feet—clams do have feet although only one foot per clam—will be leathery. If allowed to boil, the feet become so tough that they could almost be used as light armor plate. It is best, therefore, to cut off and discard the clam's foot before cooking the clam. This may seem a waste; but what is lost on clams is saved on toothpicks. The clam's foot is a narrow area shaped like the blade of some halberds. The tines of a fork will penetrate it with difficulty. If not recognized by sight, a clam's foot can be identified by a kind of probing operation. Separate from the rest of the clam with a sharp knife.

You can spare yourself a study of the clam's anatomy and a probe for its foot and save much time into the bargain by mixing two commercial products. The results are not so rewarding as the traditional version (II) but will make a good and filling meal.

I. Clam Chowder Miles Standish (*Quick Version*)

(*Serves 4*)

4 cans Snow's clam chowder (15 oz. each)
2 cans Snow's minced clams (17½ oz. each)
1½ cups milk
2 teaspoons freshly ground pepper
4 tablespoons butter

Put the clam chowder in the top of a double boiler over hot water. Drain minced clams, discarding liquid. Add clams, milk, pepper, and butter to the clam chowder. Heat over water until butter is melted and the chowder is hot through. This chowder will be ready to serve in about twenty minutes.

II. Clam Chowder Miles Standish (*Traditional Version*)

(*Serves 4*)

2 medium potatoes
1 medium onion
4 celery tops with leaves
4 ounces salt pork
2 quarts shucked clams with juice
1½ cups cream
1½ cups milk
4 tablespoons butter
2 teaspoons salt
1 teaspoon freshly ground pepper

Peel and dice potatoes small to make two cups. Chop onion coarsely. Mince celery tops, including leaves, fine. Remove rind and cut salt pork into half-inch dice. Set all aside. Drain clams, reserving juice. Remove and discard clams' feet. Chop clams coarsely. Put clam juice, 1 cup water, and chopped clams in a heavy saucepan, cover, and bring to a boil over very high flame. Strain immediately, reserving both clams and liquid. Meanwhile put pork dice into a soup kettle and cook over a high flame, turning from time to time, until pork is light brown on all sides. Put in chopped onion and cook, stirring occasionally, until onion is soft but not brown. Add clam broth, diced potatoes, and celery, cover, bring to a boil over moderate heat, and simmer until potatoes are tender but not mushy, about twenty minutes. Add cream, milk, butter, salt, and pepper. Bring to a boil, reduce heat, add chopped clams, stir well, and serve in hot soup plates.

SUGGESTED MENU

With either recipe, hard oyster crackers called "Trentons" will provide the "bread." King Cole Slaw (G) is the proper salad. Almost any dry white wine would be acceptable. Bernkasetler Riesling is probably the best but other similar wines could well be substituted.

FISH CHOWDER MASSTEX

(*Serves 4*)

Many years ago when I was young, obnoxious, and had not practiced baby farming, I asked my father—a very wise man—to mail two letters for me. One was directed to San Antonio, the other to Marblehead. My father glanced at the addresses. He said, "You have more sense than I thought; at least you keep them well separated." The anecdote may not seem germane to fish chowder but it is, in reverse. This recipe combines two others: one from the Gulf Coast, one from New England. Red snapper and bacon are typical ingredients of Southern fish chowder; all the rest comes from Down East. Except in a culinary compendium it seems unnecessary to have two recipes for what is essentially the same dish. By combining two varieties, one recipe covers the subject. Those who are still fighting the Civil War may substitute cod for red snapper and omit the bacon.

Like some people I know but who shall remain anonymous, red snappers have very large heads. When you go to your fishmonger, have him fillet the fish, throwing away the head but giving you the tail and all other bones to make a total of two pounds. You will still have to pay for the head but that cost is more than offset by your not having to dispose of it later, a task roughly equivalent to the fifth labor of Heracles. This recipe yields enough for four moderately hungry people. For very hungry people, increase the ingredients by one half.

This chowder takes only about an hour and a half to prepare. The time can be shortened, however, by substituting two bottles—total fifteen ounces—clam juice for the fish stock. The juice adds a certain tanginess which some may prefer. Follow the recipe exactly except for preparing fish stock.

1 medium onion
3 medium potatoes
4 slices bacon
2 pounds red snapper
2 ounces salt pork
2 cups milk
1 teaspoon salt
1 teaspoon freshly ground black pepper
2 tablespoons butter
oysterettes

Peel onion, cut in half, and slice very thin. Peel potatoes and slice equally thin to make two cups. Set both aside. Blanch bacon in boiling water for three minutes, drain, and put bacon on paper towels to dry. Put fish bones and tail in a saucepan, add two cups water. Bring to a boil, reduce heat, cover, and simmer twenty minutes. While fish bones simmer, fry bacon in a skillet until done. Cut fish fillets into one-inch pieces. Put potato slices in a saucepan, cover with water, and parboil for five minutes. Chop the salt pork into half-inch cubes. Drain bacon, discarding fat, and crumble, not too small. Drain potato slices, discarding liquid, and set aside. By now the fish bones should be done. Drain, reserving the stock, remove any fish from bones, and discard bones. Place cubed pork in a soup kettle and cook over a moderate flame, turning constantly, until pork is light brown on all sides. Add onion slices and continue to cook until onions are transparent, about fifteen minutes. Add parboiled potatoes and one cup of fish stock (or clam juice). Cover and simmer for ten minutes. While soup is simmering, scald milk. Add salt, pepper, butter, and scalded milk to kettle. Bring once more to a boil and serve in hot soup plates, with a plentiful supply of oysterettes for dunking.

SUGGESTED MENU

The small oyster crackers served with the soup obviate the need for other bread. Almost any light salad follows the chowder well. Perhaps one of the more complicated mixed green salads would be best. Add a few cherry tomatoes, a bit of chopped cucumber, some scallions, a small diced raw turnip, and a small, thinly sliced carrot to the lettuce and mix with French dressing (G). This would do well indeed. While chowders originated in France, *ita uti supra demonstravimus,* this recipe is so thoroughly American that an American wine should be served with it. Guild makes a good "Rhine" white wine, which should be served chilled. Any other dry white wine of similar quality is acceptable.

SOFT CRAB GUMBO MARYLAND

(*Serves 4*)

Certain parts of Maryland, particularly the counties along the shores of the Chesapeake Bay, are famous for a crab soup which bears some resemblance to the following recipe. The soup, however, is made with hard crabs, and places a horrendous burden on the diner. Peterkin Pepit once spent a long weekend at the estate of a friend in one of the Eastern Shore counties. The place was an old plantation, called "Shad's Spectre," because the ghosts of all the shad roe eaten there were believed to haunt the manor-house kitchens. One's imagination boggles at what this could mean, if true. In any cvcnt, Peterkin was served soft crabs and fresh corn for lunch and found them delicious.

A day or two later the luncheon consisted of crab soup. Among the other ingredients was a whole hard crab in each serving. Unless you have tried to eat a whole steamed crab at a formal meal with only your fingers and a spoon, you can have no idea of the effort involved or the potentiality for disaster. Steamed crabs are difficult enough to master when served with an ice mallet, a chopping block covered with newspapers, and a lobster pick. The whole meal should be eaten in a bathing suit and under a shower. At least so Peterkin described the operation. He wondered aloud to his host whether one could not make the same soup and use soft crabs instead of hard. He was met with a stony stare, and a few moments of cold silence. "My dear fellow," the host said, "one simply does not eat soft crabs any way except sautéed in butter with salt, pepper, and a bit of lemon juice. Any other way of preparing them is culinary lunacy." Peterkin Pepit is a conservative, but his own idea appealed to him as much as the hard crabs had embarrassed him. He devised the following recipe. By adding a few pods of okra and calling the dish a gumbo, he sought to mollify his erstwhile host and still provide a soup which could be eaten at the table with clean hands, a pure heart, and decorum. The soup is good, but I understand Peterkin was never invited back to Shad's Spectre.

This gumbo is one of those borderline cases. As noted in previous soups, it can be prepared by skillful hands and a concentrated mind in just over an hour. With a little practice, the time could be reduced.

2 ears fresh corn
4 jumbo soft-shell crabs
6 tablespoons butter
1 small onion
2 medium tomatoes
¼ pound okra
1 teaspoon salt

½ green pepper
3 pints fish stock
3 tablespoons raw rice
½ teaspoon freshly ground black pepper
½ teaspoon cayenne pepper

Clean corn and cook for five minutes in rapidly boiling water. Drain, and allow to cool. While corn is cooking, clean the crabs. Scrape kernels from corn cobs, discard cobs. Place butter in a skillet, melt, and sauté the crabs over a brisk fire, turning once, until crisp on the outside and done through, about fifteen minutes. Remove crabs to a plate, retaining butter in skillet. Remove legs and claws of crabs, and keep in a warm place for garnish. Cut the remainder of the crabs into small bite-sized pieces. Chop the onion and the green pepper small, and sauté in the skillet until soft. Transfer contents of skillet, scraping all residue off bottom, into a large, heavy saucepan, or soup kettle. Add stock and rice, cover, bring to a boil, and simmer over medium flame for twenty minutes until rice is cooked. While rice is cooking, peel the tomatoes, and chop them into half-inch pieces. Scrape the okra and cut it into half-inch slices. When rice is done, add the tomatoes and okra to the saucepan. Season with salt, pepper, and cayenne. Cover and simmer fifteen minutes. Put in the crab pieces and corn kernels, simmer five minutes, and taste. Correct the seasoning; it will probably need more salt. Stir. Place contents of saucepan in hot soup plates or a hot tureen. Garnish with the crab claws and legs. Serve very hot.

SUGGESTED MENU

Two kinds of bread are ideal with the gumbo: Maryland Beaten Biscuits (G) or corn sticks. Of the two, Peterkin prefers the former. King Cole Slaw (G) is an obvious choice for a salad. Cole slaw and seafood are always a good combination. On the other hand, Pontalba Salad (G) from New Orleans is a natural with any gumbo. Gumbo deserves a rather special treatment in the wine department. A Schloss Johannisberger or Charles Heidsieck champagne is indicated here.

PURÉE OF CLAMS BAR HARBOR

(Serves 4)

The Peterkin Pepit Papers reveal that he was very fond of Bar Harbor. "It is a pleasant place," he wrote (Diary, Vol. XXVI), "and its name is most appealing to one of my disposition. I find it indeed a harbour from the raw, cold, biting blasts of life; 'Harbour' preceded by the word 'Bar' gives me faith in the future, provides hope for *hoi polloi,* and raises in me a shade of charity for all mankind. Then, too, these lowly fishermen do a multitude of fine things with clams." As usual, his judgment was sound. This clam soup can be described in one word: sumptuous. It is also very rich. While it had its origin in Maine, on its way south it went through several sea changes, some of them expensive. Few Yankees—whose thriftiness is exceeded only by that of the Scots—would, for example, throw away some three pints of ground, edible clams. A Marylander did, not because he was a wastrel—although disagreement exists on that score—but because he wanted a purée and not a chowder. The clams are discarded for the purée only. They can be used to make a very fine canapé by spreading them on small thin slices of pumpernickel or rye bread, and garnishing each with a small sprig of watercress.

Comparatively speaking, Purée of Clam Bar Harbor does not require an inordinate amount of time, but a quicker and somewhat easier version is possible. Candor compels me to concede that the "fast" of it is as good as the "fancy" of it.

The fancy variety of Purée of Clam, which was Pepit's favorite, was made in his Bar Harbor cottage as in II. The recipe is based on shucked clams without juice. If clams come with juice, three pints of "dry" clams are still required. Be sure to simmer the clams and celery in the juice instead of in water.

I. Purée of Clams Bar Harbor (*Quick Version*)

(*Serves 4*)

8 medium stalks celery
8 large scallions
6 tablespoons butter
2 quarts milk
6 tablespoons sifted flour
4 cans Snow's minced clams (7½ oz. each)
1 teaspoon salt
2 teaspoons freshly ground pepper
paprika

Remove and discard celery leaves. Mince celery and scallions, including part of the green tops. Place butter in a heavy saucepan and cook minced celery and scallions slowly until both are soft. Meanwhile, scald three pints of milk. Add flour to saucepan and blend into a roux (G), cooking slowly and stirring from time to time for five minutes. Drain clams, reserving juice. When roux has cooked, gradually add scalded milk, and reserved clam juice. Put in minced clams and season with salt and pepper. Over a low heat, beat with a large wire whisk until the soup is smooth, and gradually bring to a simmer, but do not allow to boil. Remove from fire and allow to stand for five minutes. Put through a blender at high speed for thirty seconds. While soup is still warm, put it through a medium-coarse kitchen strainer. Discard residue in strainer. The yield will be a thick purée. Return it to the saucepan, and thin to desired consistency with remaining milk. A pint of milk should be enough. Taste, and correct seasoning. Heat gently to a simmer and serve in hot plates. Garnish with paprika.

II. Purée of Clams Bar Harbor (*Traditional Version*)

(*Serves 4*)

3 pints shucked clams
8 stalks celery
8 large scallions
6 tablespoons butter
6 tablespoons flour
2 quarts milk
1 teaspoon salt
2 teaspoons freshly ground pepper
paprika

Put clams, followed by the celery through finest blade of a meat grinder, and set aside. Mince scallions very fine. Put butter in a large, heavy saucepan, melt, and add minced scallions. Sauté until scallions are soft. Add flour and make a roux (G). While roux is cooking, put clams and celery into another saucepan, barely cover with hot water (or hot clam juice) and simmer for three minutes. Meanwhile, scald milk. Add milk to roux and heat slowly, stirring frequently, to bring to desired consistency. Strain clams and celery, and add both to saucepan. Season with salt, and pepper. Bring just to a simmer, remove from fire, and allow to cool for about an hour. Put into blender and operate at moderate speed for approximately thirty seconds. Strain through a kitchen sieve, discarding solids left in strainer. Put soup in a bowl, cover, and refrigerate overnight. Place soup in double boiler, heat over water, and garnish with paprika just before serving. If soup is too thick after standing, thin with a little milk before heating. Do not boil.

SUGGESTED MENU

Maryland Beaten Biscuits (G) are obviously right with this purée; Hofburg Salad (G) would follow it well. One of the New York light white, and dry table wines would be a good choice.

PURÉE OF CRAB WICOMICO COUNTY, MARYLAND

(*Serves 4*)

One of the few people, or indeed subjects, over which Pepit and Dottle ever had their respective noses out of joint was a woman known to both of them as "The High Priestess." Both gentlemen were most reticent on the subject and I never learned her real name. Their tiff was not open and was known only to a few of their intimate friends. I have never been able to ascertain whether this was a case of normal jealousy or whether it was because she gave the following recipe to Dottle without sharing it at the same time with Pepit. Dottle was a great ploy player. The fact that he was able to serve Pepit this delicious soup unquestionably was as good for his ego as it was annoying to Pepit. Being sensible men, they never allowed this incident to cause a rift in their friendship. If you wish to taste a soup which between lesser men might have created a schism, try the following recipe. An hour is ample time for its preparation.

1 bunch watercress
4 tablespoons butter
4 tablespoons sifted flour
3 cups fish stock (p. 7)
¾ teaspoon powdered sage
1 cup dry white wine
4 cups milk
2 pounds lump crabmeat
1½ teaspoons freshly ground pepper
salt
paprika

Wash watercress and strip off enough leaves to make one and a half generous cups. Discard stems. Put butter in a heavy saucepan, melt, and add flour to make a roux (G). While roux is cooking, heat fish stock. When roux is done, add fish stock slowly to saucepan, stirring the while to make a sauce. Heat sauce over a low flame, stirring from time to time until it begins to bubble. Now add the watercress leaves, and powdered sage. Cook over moderate heat, stirring frequently. When soup starts to simmer around the edges, add wine and two cups milk. While contents of pan are coming to a boil again, select twenty-four best crab lumps and reserve. When contents of pan begin to simmer, add remaining crabmeat and stir it in well. Cover saucepan and remove from fire. Allow to cool for five minutes. Put contents of pan into blender and blend at high speed for thirty seconds. Return to saucepan and add remaining milk. Put through blender again at same speed. Return soup to saucepan, cover, and bring slowly once again to a simmer. Taste soup and correct seasoning with salt or pepper. If soup is too thick, thin with milk. Serve in hot soup plates garnished with reserved crabmeat and sprinkled lightly with paprika.

SUGGESTED MENU

The obvious bread is Maryland Beaten Biscuit (G). This is a very rich soup and should have one of the lighter salads. One choice would be Salade Flandre (G). A delicate white wine, such as a Piesporter, would go well with the crab and enhance rather than cover its taste.

OYSTER STEW HARFORD

(*Serves* 2)

This oyster stew, from an old family recipe, has appeared in two cookbooks but it is so good that it bears repetition even in a third, especially when that third is devoted to hearty soups for the gourmet's luncheon or supper. The recipe also illustrates a rather interesting culinary point: even the best cooks will not always achieve the expected result if given the ingredients of a new dish but no suggestions on preparation.

One of the best restaurants in New York City is the Baroque, which has been at the same spot on East Fifty-third Street for a quarter of a century. Its food is legendary. A number of years ago I asked Josef, the proprietor, if his chef would prepare an oyster stew for me if I gave him the list of ingredients. Josef said he would be delighted, and noted down the recipe's table of contents as listed below under II. I was to return two days later for the tasting.

The dish was served. Josef, two waiters, and one of the captains hovered over me. I tasted. It was magnificent. It was also totally unexpected. The consistency was different, the appearance was different, and the taste subtly altered. The chef had puréed the vegetables after cooking them in butter. It was an interesting and rewarding experiment, one you might like to try.

The original family recipe (II) can be made in about an hour and a half, which is not inordinately long. A number of years ago, however, I devised a shorter method so that a friend of mine and I could have oyster stew for lunch. The friend has the same inordinate lust after oysters as do I. We had no Bailey's Beach—a famous source of oysters—to walk, but the Washington waterfront provided a plentiful supply of oysters. Whenever we could slip away from our respective offices, we sped to the wharf, bought a quart of oysters, and hied ourselves to my domicile, where we made the quick version (I). Under no circumstances whatever, in either version, must the dish be allowed to boil. Recipe I also saves calories, if you care about that sort of thing. Never wash shucked oysters.

I. Oyster Stew Harford (*Quick Version*)

(*Serves* 2)

2 tablespoons instant onions (Spice Island by choice)
1 quart large fresh oysters
1½ cups milk
3 tablespoons butter
4 teaspoons celery seed
2 teaspoons minced parsley (Spice Island)
salt
pepper
paprika

Place the instant onions in a small bowl and cover them with water. Stir well and let the onions hydrate. Place the oysters in a skillet and cook them over the lowest heat possible, stirring occasionally. Place the milk in a small saucepan, add the butter, the celery seed, and the parsley. Heat slowly, gently agitating from time to time, until the butter has melted. By now, about ten minutes, the onions should have absorbed enough water, and the oysters should have begun to simmer. Add the onions to the saucepan, stir well, and season with salt and pepper to taste. Pour the contents of the saucepan into the skillet, raise the heat, and stir constantly with a large spoon until the oysters' edges curl, about ten minutes. Place in hot soup plates, sprinkle with paprika, and serve at once.

II. Oyster Stew Harford (*Traditional Version*)

(*Serves* 2)

1 quart large fresh oysters
1 medium onion
2 tender medium stalks celery, including leaves
½ tart apple
6 tablespoons butter
½ pint light cream
salt
pepper
paprika

Drain liquid from oysters into a large skillet and set the oysters aside.

Dice the onion, the celery—including the leaves—and the apple. You may peel the apple if you like; I prefer it unpeeled. Add the butter to the oyster liquor, and heat very gently. When the contents of the skillet are hot, add the diced vegetables and fruit, and continue to cook over a low flame, stirring frequently, until the celery and onion are soft. Pour in the cream and season with salt and pepper to taste. Watch the skillet carefully and as soon as bubbles appear around the edges of the liquid—can liquids hold an edge?—put in the oysters. Now you stir constantly, but gently, with a large spoon. Under no circumstances allow the contents of the skillet to boil. If you do, even for a few seconds, you might as well throw the whole thing down the garbage-disposal, and go to the nearest hamburger stand for lunch. You deserve to. When the oysters are plump, firm, and their edges curl, they are done. The stew should be placed in hot soup plates, garnished with paprika, and eaten at once. If you overcook oysters, they get hard, shrink, and lose their first fine careless rapture, and so do you.

SUGGESTED MENU

With both stews you should serve oysterettes, which are—a few at a time—daintily dropped into the stew by each diner and allowed to swim around contentedly with the bivalves. Salads really do not go with this stew. You can have King Cole Slaw (G), but I prefer a quarter of a small cabbage served raw with salt and pepper on the side. The cabbage pretty much has to be eaten with the fingers. Wine? Yes, and Chablis, naturally.

PHILADELPHIA PEPPER POT

(*Serves 4*)

This famous Pennsylvania soup is made with tripe and time—it takes two days and there is no quick version. Tripe is the lining of a cow's stomach. Legend has it that the dish was invented by a cook in the Continental Army during the terrible winter at Valley Forge and that the soup saved the Revolution. I don't believe it. No army cook, except possibly one attached to Lafayette's own mess, ever had the imagination or skill to create so succulent a soup.

I prefer to believe, with no foundation I admit, that the genius of Benjamin Franklin was responsible. In my mind's eye, I can see very clearly what may have happened. While Franklin was a diplomatist in France seeking aid for the struggling Colonies he employed many stratagems to effect his purpose. I doubt that he would have neglected to appeal to the French love of food. Perhaps while walking one day in Paris he chanced upon a bargain in tripe. Unable to resist the bargain—after all it was he who said "a penny a day is a pound a year" (actually it is one pound, sixteen shillings, and five pence)—he bought some tripe. What to do with the purchase would not have given that mind ten minutes' concern. By the time he had returned from the walk he had doubtless worked up a recipe. One can imagine the paeans of praise from the guests when it was first served at an intimate dinner presumably made up of the more influential advisors of Louis XVI. One can also imagine Franklin's well-known sly but self-effacing smile and perhaps some remark that the dish was just an ordinary one native to Philadelphia and was called—his cook used too much pepper —"pepper pot." If the Colonists represented by Mr. Franklin could produce such a dish they obviously qualified for foreign aid. It is unlikely that such an event occurred, but I prefer to think that Philadephia Pepper Pot was more influential in helping to bring France into the conflict on the side of the Colonies than was the victory at Saratoga. You can decide for yourself but not, at least, until you have tasted the soup itself.

The soup takes two days or approximately eighteen hours to make. For much of that time, however, it may be left unattended. Once the two pots have begun to simmer they need scant watching for five hours. Later, both broths must be refrigerated overnight or for at least eight hours. Actual time in the kitchen amounts to about three hours; even that can be reduced by speedy preparation. Be sure your butcher provides a cracked marrow bone with plenty of marrow in it. The marrow may be removed with the bowl or handle of a spoon or a dull knife, depending on the shape of the space to be emptied. All recipes should be read through at least once before being attempted for the first time. This recipe should be read at least twice.

As noted above, no short cuts are possible with Philadelphia Pepper Pot. You take the time to make it, you forgo it, or you take it out of a can. Some of the commercially made versions are quite good. They can be improved by the addition of minced parsley and Scotch Bonnet (G) at the last minute. The soup is well worth the time and trouble, and it will keep, refrigerated, for several days. The dumplings, however, must be made fresh.

First Day

1 pound tripe
1 medium onion
1 small carrot
bouquet garni (G)
(1 bay leaf 2 sprigs parsley
½ teaspoon dry thyme)

1 small marrow bone, cracked
1 veal knuckle
¼ teaspoon cracked red pepper
½ teaspoon allspice
4 cloves

Wash tripe well, put in soup kettle, add five quarts water. Bring to a boil, reduce heat and simmer, covered, seven hours. Peel and slice onion and carrot. Make bouquet garni. Remove marrow from bone, and place in a skillet. Melt marrow, put in onion and carrot slices and cook over a moderate flame, stirring occasionally, until onion is soft. Meanwhile put veal knuckle into another soup kettle or large saucepan; cover with five quarts water. Put the marrow bone in with the veal, add contents of skillet, the bouquet garni, cracked pepper, allspice, and cloves. Bring to a boil, cover, and simmer five hours. When veal knuckle is finished cooking, remove pot from fire and allow to cool. When veal can be handled comfortably, remove, and cut off and chop small any edible meat; reserve. Discard all bones. Discard bouquet garni. Strain broth; place in a mixing bowl, cover, and put in refrigerator. When tripe is done remove kettle from fire and set aside until meat is cool enough to handle. Dice it. Place broth, covered, in refrigerator. Mix chopped tripe and veal, if any, and stow in refrigerator. All three bowls should remain in refrigerator overnight or at least eight hours.

Second Day

2 medium potatoes
1 teaspoon marjoram
2 teaspoons salt
1 teaspoon black pepper
2 tablespoons minced parsley
½ cup flour
1 teaspoon baking powder
⅛ teaspoon salt
1½ teaspoons Crisco or other soft shortening
4 tablespoons milk
1 teaspoon Scotch Bonnet (G)

Remove bowls from refrigerator. Skim and discard fat from both broths. Combine broths in a large soup kettle. Peel and dice the potatoes small and add to kettle. Put in the tripe and veal, the marjoram, salt, and pepper. Bring to a boil, and simmer, covered, forty-five minutes. While soup simmers, mince parsley. Combine flour, baking powder, and salt. Sift them into a bowl, add shortening and cut in or mix well with fingers. After soup has simmered for forty-two minutes, add milk to flour mixture and stir well with a fork to make a dough for dumplings. Bring soup to a rapid boil and put in the dumpling dough, a half teaspoon at a time. Add minced parsley, and Scotch Bonnet. Reduce heat, and simmer, covered, for fifteen minutes. The soup is now ready to serve.

SUGGESTED MENU

Bread will be neither needed nor missed with a dumplinged—Fowler forgive me—soup. A Hofburg Salad (G) would make a pleasing accompanying or following dish. A good, full-bodied red wine would enhance the meal.

CREAM OF MUSHROOM SOUP

(*Serves 4*)

Not much can be said, really, about Cream of Mushroom Soup. To write about it is a bit like being a toastmaster at a banquet introducing the principal speaker. The toastmaster starts out by remarking that very little need be said about such a distinguished guest. He then goes on for half an hour extolling the gentleman's merits, all of which are well known to everyone else in the room. Finally he mentions the speaker's name as though none of the other guests had ever heard of him and will be inordinately surprised and pleased to learn who is to address them. It is quite a trick if you can do it. So, having written that, one can go on for two pages extolling the merits of Mushroom Soup, all well known to any cook. One should be content with less space. The commercial product, properly used, makes: (a) a good beginning to a meal; and (b) a fine basis for sauces with certain meat and fowl.

In making it from scratch, the chef should avoid the deadly amanita, a toadstool, if he ever wants to make mushroom or any other kind of soup again.

1 pound fresh mushrooms
5 tablespoons butter
3 cups Béchamel Sauce (G)
1 cup beef stock
1 cup cream
1 cup milk
1 teaspoon salt
½ teaspoon freshly ground white pepper

Wash mushrooms. Remove stems from all, and reserve four of the smallest caps. Cut off and discard the bottom of each stem. Dice stems very fine, discarding any that are "woody." Dice the caps. Melt four tablespoons butter in a heavy skillet, add the diced mushrooms and cook slowly for about fifteen minutes, turning frequently. With a sharp knife, flute the reserved caps, melt the remaining tablespoon butter in a small skillet and cook the caps on both sides until done. Set aside. Put the Béchamel Sauce in a large saucepan, add the diced mushrooms, pour in the stock, and bring to a simmer. Remove from fire and pour into a blender. Blend at high speed for half a minute. Return to saucepan, add cream, milk, salt, and pepper. Stir well and heat very slowly. When soup is hot through, taste, correct seasoning, and pour into hot soup plates. Garnish each plate with one of the reserved caps, convex side up to insure flotation. Serve at once.

The key to preparation time lies in the Béchamel Sauce. If it is ready, the soup can be done in about three-quarters of an hour. If it is not ready, the time will necessarily be increased.

SUGGESTED MENU

For bread, Brigid's (G) would do very nicely, as would Salade Flandre (G). If you have a taste for slightly sweet wine, a dry sauterne might be acceptable, otherwise, one of the wines from the Rheingau would complement and compliment the meal.

CREAM OF TOMATO SOUP

(*Serves 4*)

Cream of Tomato Soup is included in this book of recipes for two reasons. It is one of the most widely known American soups; and it is essential if you wish to make Peterkin Pepit's version of Potage Mongole (page 118). To be completely honest, as usual, I think the various commercial varieties are to be preferred. If you must make your own, the following recipe is suggested. It takes about an hour of rapid work. The recipe yields a soup which is considerably lighter in color than commercial tomato soup. You may darken it by using red vegetable coloring. A quarter teaspoon of coloring will make a light pink product. A half teaspoon results in a lavender soup. It tastes good but looks ghastly.

8 medium tomatoes
1 medium leek
1 small stalk celery with leaves
1 small bay leaf
¼ teaspoon brown sugar
¼ teaspoon ground cloves
4 tablespoons butter
4 tablespoons flour
2¼ cups milk
½ cup cream
salt
black pepper
parsley
small croutons (G)

Stem and peel tomatoes. Chop them coarsely. Mince leek and celery to make one-fourth cup each. In a large saucepan place the chopped tomatoes, leek, celery, bay leaf, sugar, and cloves. Cover the whole with water and simmer uncovered until the tomatoes are mushy, about fifteen minutes. Meanwhile, melt butter in another large saucepan. Add flour and make a roux (G). While roux is cooking, scald milk and cream in a third saucepan. (You need a scullery maid if you make Cream of Tomato Soup.) When roux is done, add contents of third saucepan to the roux and stir over low heat with a wire whisk to break up lumps. Continue to cook over a low flame until the contents begin to bubble. Cover, and remove from fire. When tomatoes are done, drain through kitchen strainer, reserving juice. Put contents of strainer into a blender. Add half a cup reserved juice and blend at high speed for fifteen seconds. Add contents of blender to the cream sauce. Stir well, and thin to desired consistency with remaining juice. Bring to a boil once more over a low flame; taste, and correct seasoning with salt and pepper. Garnish with minced parsley and serve with croutons on the side.

SUGGESTED MENU

With croutons no additional bread is necessary. Almost any light salad will go with this soup. Tomatoes, of course, should not be a part of the salad. A light, dry white wine from California would be a good beverage.

VICHYSSOISE

(*Serves 4*)

The great French cook Louis Diat is credited with creating this magnificent cold soup when he was chef at the newly opened Ritz Hotel in New York City. Certainly it is usually accepted as an American contribution to gourmet dining. But several other chefs have claimed it. One, and perhaps the most vociferous, was at the Savoy in London shortly after World War II. One of the directors of the hotel returned from a trip to the United States, and sent for his chef. The director, a charming and soft-spoken gentleman, explained that he had found a fine soup on his trip and thought it should be added to the Savoy's menu. When he read the recipe from his notes, the chef, who stood six feet three and was wearing a three foot chef's hat expanded as though he were about to have apoplexy. His hat almost went through the ceiling. He announced in broken English but with a brazen voice that he, and he alone had first introduced this leek and potato soup, that he was the originator, the inventor, and the concocter, and if anyone else claimed it, the claimant was . . . well, the French have a number of words for it, modified by a whole army of adjectives.

Who the actual inventor was is academic. It is one of the world's great cold soups. Only two or three are its peers. It makes a magnificent luncheon or supper, and served in cream soup dishes rather than larger soup plates, it provides one of the finest soup courses known for a dinner in warm weather. It is sometimes served hot but is at its best when well chilled.

It is quite possible to make this cream of all cream soups quite rapidly, but how much time you save between the start and the eating is questionable. The soup still must be chilled before it is served. The recipe as described below takes something less than an hour. The test recipe was completed at ten-fifteen in the morning, immediately placed in the refrigerator, and was still warm three hours later. I served it for dinner at eight, and it was just about the right temperature. This first recipe (I) is faster and easier than the following one (II). Whichever you use, the soup is really best made the night before it is to be served so it has ample time to chill. The chilling time can be considerably reduced, of course, by putting the soup in a freezer, for a short time—but do not allow it to freeze.

I. Vichyssoise

(*Quick Version*)

(*Serves* 4)

- 2 cans Campbell's frozen Cream of Potato Soup (10 oz. each)
- 5 cups chicken stock, unsalted
- 2 packages Knorr's Cream of Leek Soup mix (1¾ oz. each)
- 2 cups milk
- 1 teaspoon freshly ground white pepper
- 4 tablespoons chopped chives

Thaw potato soup according to directions on the can. Bring chicken stock to a light boil in a saucepan. Gradually stir in the leek soup mix, cover, and simmer gently for five minutes. Place potato soup in another saucepan, add milk, mix well, and bring to a simmer, stirring frequently with a wire whisk to prevent lumping. Mix the contents of the two saucepans, add pepper, and stir well with the whisk. Pour into a blender and operate it at high speed for twenty seconds—you will probably have to make two or more runs with the blender. Pour through a kitchen strainer into a mixing bowl, cover, and place in refrigerator to chill. Just before serving, garnish each plate with a generous quantity of fresh, chopped chives.

II. Vichyssoise (*Traditional Version*)

(*Serves 4*)

1 bunch leeks
1 bunch scallions
3 tablespoons butter
3 largish potatoes
1 quart chicken stock
1 tablespoon salt
3 cups milk
2 teaspoons freshly ground white pepper
1½ cups heavy cream
fresh chives

Wash leeks and scallions and remove outer layer of each. Slice white part of each very thin, to make about three cups. Place butter in a heavy saucepan, melt, and add sliced leeks and scallions. Cook over a low heat, stirring now and again. While leeks and scallions cook, peel potatoes and slice very thin. When leeks and scallions are golden, add stock, potato slices, and salt. Cover, and simmer forty minutes, or until potatoes are tender. Put contents of saucepan in blender and operate at high speed for twenty seconds. Return to saucepan, add milk and white pepper, bring slowly to a simmer but do not let boil. Remove from fire, stir in cream, correct seasoning. Transfer to a bowl, and place in refrigerator until well chilled. Just before serving, mince enough fresh chives to fill three tablespoons. Pour soup into well-chilled soup plates, sprinkle each plate with chives, and serve.

SUGGESTED MENU

Cold artichokes after the soup are excellent, particularly if served with Vinaigrette Dressing (G). Although a little heretical, Brigid's Bread (G) would add flavor to the soup if only because of the caraway seed. A light, very dry white wine from the Rhine would make this a truly international lunch.

CHICKEN BROTH IN ERROR

(*Serves 4*)

As my old friend, Dr. F. X. Dottle, the eminent orthopedist and gastronome, used to say, "Most great discoveries were mistakes." He was speaking of the discovery of new drugs by people who were seeking something else. His aphorism is applicable to the kitchen. One recalls the accidental burning down of a house which led to the discovery of roast pig. A similar—albeit less expensive—error resulted in this fine broth. Dottle himself made the error. I am happy to say I made the discovery.

The good doctor, a bachelor, invited three friends to dine from a menu built around chicken tarragon. The recipe called for four chicken breasts. His error lay in neglecting to bone them, hence the only cooking utensil of sufficient size in his kitchen was a two-gallon cocotte. To cover the chicken required a large quantity of liquid, in this case chicken broth. After the meal, he wondered aloud what he was going to do with all the fine broth. The heavy tarragon seasoning rendered it unsuitable for use as a cooking broth or marinade. It might make a good soup, I suggested. After all, it was a double bouillon redoubled. Next day's lunch gave us the recipe designated as II.

If you are going to have chicken tarragon, it takes a comparatively short time to make the soup later, particularly if you plan ahead and cook more chicken then you need immediately. If, however, you wish to make the chicken broth quickly and without having had chicken tarragon, I suggest the following rapid method (I). For those who wish to follow the "error" of Dr. Dottle without having chicken tarragon earlier, method II is commended to their attention. When making broth, of course, the chicken should not be boned.

I. Chicken Broth in Error (*Quick Version*)

(*Serves 4*)

1 medium can or jar cooked chicken (5½ oz.)
8 cups chicken stock
2 cups cooked rice
1 generous tablespoon tarragon
1 teaspoon salt
1 teaspoon black pepper

Chop the chicken fine and place all ingredients in a heavy saucepan. Bring to a boil. Reduce heat and simmer about ten minutes, or long enough to heat everything thoroughly.

II. Chicken Broth in Error (*Traditional Version*)

(*Serves 4*)

2 medium chicken breasts
1 generous tablespoon dried tarragon
1 teaspoon salt
1 teaspoon freshly ground pepper
8 cups chicken broth
2 cups cooked rice

Place the chicken in a large, heavy saucepan or soup kettle. Sprinkle with tarragon, salt, and pepper. Let stand about fifteen minutes. Pour in the broth, cover, and bring to a boil over high heat. Reduce flame and simmer urgently for one hour. Remove chicken, and set aside. Add rice to the saucepan. Cut chicken into large dice. Return to broth. Taste, and adjust seasoning. Return saucepan to the fire, and simmer very gently, to heat everything thoroughly, about five minutes. All errors now stand corrected and you have a healthful and a very good soup.

SUGGESTED MENU

This is a fairly light soup, despite the rice. Serve a reasonably substantial salad, but no bread. A cold artichoke salad with Vinaigrette Dressing (G) should do very nicely. A light, very dry white wine would add to the meal.

CREAM OF CHICKEN CHESAPEAKE

(*Serves 4*)

Cream of Chicken Soup is known, under one name or another, throughout most of the gastronomic world. This recipe stems from a very young man's first trip alone on the water. The water was the Chesapeake Bay and he was traveling from Baltimore to Norfolk on the Baltimore Steam Packet Company's *City of Richmond,* to see a girl, naturally. In those days the "Old Bay Line," as it was known to its many regular and irregular passengers, had been operating between Baltimore, Old Point Comfort, and Norfolk for almost a hundred years. Its reputation for comfort, service, and food was equal to that of any other similar transportation company in the United States, including the more famous Fall River Line, which had an additional reputation. The young man was so full of anticipation, which later proved to have been wishful thinking, that he spent most of the night on the deck. There he silently assisted the unwitting lookout on the bow by quietly reciting to himself Newbolt's *The King's Highway* and similar appropriate verse. When the vessel docked at about six the next morning, he was very hungry. It was far too early to go ashore and phone the young lady. He repaired to the dining saloon. On the advice of a benevolent and understanding steward he had creamed chicken hash. It was the best breakfast he had ever had. That he remembers it some forty years and hundreds of memorable breakfasts later would indicate that the hash "had something." It did: a generous quantity of very finely minced green pepper. And it is the green pepper which sets this Cream of Chicken Soup apart from most others.

The recollection of that breakfast led to the invention of the traditional version of the soup. A swifter method is described immediately below. It goes like this.

I. Cream of Chicken Chesapeake (*Quick Version*)

(*Serves 4*)

1 large green pepper
3 teaspoons instant chicken broth mix
½ cup parsley leaves, loose
1 can cooked chicken (5½ oz.), white meat preferably
3 cans condensed Cream of Chicken Soup (10 oz. each)
3 cups milk
freshly ground pepper

Clean and mince the green pepper. Put a cup and a half of water into a small saucepan. Bring to a boil, add the chicken broth mix and stir well. Put in the minced green pepper and allow to simmer, uncovered, until broth has been reduced to one cup and pepper is soft. Both events should occur at about the same time. While the simmering and reduction are going on, wash and mince the parsley leaves, and chop the cooked chicken into fine dice. Put canned soup into top half of double boiler, and add the contents of the small saucepan and the milk. Heat over boiling water. Just before soup starts to simmer, add the diced chicken. Bring almost to a boil, taste, and add salt if needed and at least a half teaspoon, probably a whole teaspoon, freshly ground pepper. Just before serving, garnish with the minced parsley. You may prepare this soup in a saucepan if you are willing to stand over it and stir very frequently to prevent scorching. This method will obviously require less time. If the soup is too thick, thin by adding additional milk.

II. Cream of Chicken Chesapeake (*Traditional Version*)

(*Serves 4*)

1 carrot
1 medium onion
1 large chicken breast
4 chicken legs
4 chicken thighs
12 peppercorns
3 sprigs parsley
3 celery tops
2 teaspoons salt
2 teaspoons freshly ground white pepper
1 green pepper
3 cups Béchamel Sauce (G)
½ cup heavy cream
1 tablespoon butter
2 tablespoons minced parsley

Scrape carrot and cut into one-inch lengths. Peel and quarter onion. Place chicken, carrot, and onion in a large saucepan or soup kettle. Add peppercorns, parsley, celery tops, salt, and pepper. Pour in six cups water, cover, bring to a boil, and simmer for forty minutes, or until chicken is tender. Strain, reserving both broth and chicken. Remove and discard bones and skin from chicken. Cut the chicken breast into small dice, and set aside. Chop the rest of the chicken coarsely and return to broth. While the chicken simmers, mince the green pepper small and make the Béchamel Sauce. Add the diced pepper to the broth and chicken, and simmer five minutes. Run the contents of the saucepan through a blender for one minute at high speed. Put the mixture through a strainer, forcing it through with a wooden spoon. Reserve broth and the chicken residue in strainer. (This meat has nothing further to do with the soup but, mixed with a little mayonnaise and spread on hot toast, makes a fine sandwich; it may also be used as a base for canapés.) Add reserved diced white meat and contents of saucepan to Béchamel Sauce, heat. As it starts to simmer, put in cream and butter. Do not let boil. Stir well, taste, correct seasoning if necessary, garnish with parsley, and serve very hot.

SUGGESTED MENU

A mixed green salad with French dressing (G) would be appropriate afterward. The bread with the soup should be crusty. Piesporters are recommended with chicken. Try one and learn why.

FERN SOUP

(Serves 4)

We are all indebted to my friend Hazel, of the famous Herbage (G), for this occasional soup. The word "occasional" in this sense is employed as one does the same adjective as applied to a chair. It is used only from time to time. In the case of the soup the time is whenever you have access to fiddlehead ferns.

Actually the ferns will grow in almost any temperate climate where there is a reasonable amount of moisture and dark earth. Only the tops of the ferns are used. They must be plucked while they are still tightly coiled. Once opened they are edible but the consistency is lost. The coil when plucked should be tight and hard. They should not be overcooked.

Hazel resides much of the time in an old house on Big Pipe Creek. You will recall, of course, that it was behind this stream that General George G. Meade planned to defend Pennsylvania when Robert E. Lee invaded the North in 1863. For tactical reasons the defense took place in a small Pennsylvania town called Gettysburg.

Hazel goes about making this soup as follows: obviously the preparation comes well within our time limit, about sixty minutes.

3 quarts rich chicken stock	4 egg yolks
½ cup raw rice	⅛ teaspoon cayenne pepper
3 cups fiddlehead fern tops	salt
3 lemons	pepper

Place chicken stock in a large saucepan. Add the rice and bring the stock to a simmer. Cover. Wash the fern tops thoroughly, removing all fuzz, sand, and dirt. After the chicken stock and rice have cooked thirty minutes, put in the fern tops and continue to simmer for ten minutes longer. Meanwhile, squeeze lemons and place juice in a small bowl. Add the yolks and cayenne to the lemon juice and beat until yolks and juice are well blended. Gradually add one cup of hot soup to the eggs, beating all the time. Slowly add the mixture to the saucepan; do not allow to boil. Stir violently. Taste and correct seasoning. Serve very hot.

SUGGESTED MENU

One can do no better than offer one's guests the same complements to this soup that Hazel did when I first ate it. These complements were hot muffins, Hazel's Herbage (G) and a well-chilled bottle of Frascati. It would not have occurred to me to serve an Italian wine with this soup but the combination showed her superior imagination.

TEXAS BILLIE'S BRUNSWICK STEW

(*Serves* 6)

As all right-thinking people know, proper Brunswick stew recipes invariably start with the same four words: "First shoot your squirrel." The same admonition applies to this recipe. According to James Fenimore Cooper, one of his heroes, Natty Bumppo, could shoot the eye out of a squirrel at two hundred yards, give or take a perch or two. Few people today can see a squirrel at half that distance, say the length of a football field, let alone hit him. Ol' Dan'l Boone, using a Kentucky long rifle, is alleged to have shot eyes out of squirrels with some consistency at fifty yards. If you plan to go after your own squirrels, I suggest you use a shotgun and hit the animal wherever you can and at whatever distance your weapon will carry. To hell with his eye; you will not eat it anyhow. And you can pick out the shot as you clean the squirrels. That, at least, is what Texas Billie aimed to do. She came mighty close, too. The only trouble was that the new shells she bought for her old four-ten would not go in the breech, and she had to use a borrowed gun. But she got the squirrels despite the unfamiliar weapon and the fact that she had been up until about four in the morning, drinking Canadian whiskey. She is a pretty keen gal, is Texas Billie. But this recipe was not written for her, although dedicated to her, or for other hunters. Presumably you will buy your squirrels already shot, skinned, cleaned, de-shotted, and cut up, ready to be cooked. In addition to providing the squirrels, Texas Billie, who claims the only true Brunswick stew comes from her state—a matter of argument—insisted on filé gumbo (G) as a thickener. Filé gumbo is, of course, a Choctaw seasoning usually associated with Creole cookery. It must be remembered, however, that after the fall of the Confederacy a great many people from Louisiana moved west to Texas. In any event the filé gumbo not only thickens but also flavors the soup.

Despite the admonitions in the opening paragraphs of this recipe, some people, who shall be anonymous, make Brunswick stew with chicken instead of squirrel. Before they are condemned forever to outer darkness, one must, in all candor, agree that if one is to make a quick version of this delectable dish, one must substitute already cooked chicken for squirrel. Such a "Brunswick" stew appears as I.

If you have the squirrels, the time, and the energy, you can make Texas Billie's own recipe and rejoice in the fact that you are eating an authentic Brunswick Stew.

I. Texas Billie's Brunswick Stew (*Quick Version*)

(*Serves* 6)

2 large onions
1 green pepper
2 red peppers
4 tablespoons butter
2 cans cooked tomatoes (20 oz. each)
bouquet garni (G)
  (6 sprigs parsley
  ½ teaspoon dried thyme
  12 peppercorns)
1 large can (14 oz.) boned chicken
½ pound lean cooked ham ¼ inch thick
3 pints chicken stock
½ teaspoon cayenne pepper
4 tablespoons Worcestershire sauce
1 package frozen baby lima beans (10 oz.)
1 package frozen corn kernels (10 oz.)
salt
pepper

Peel onions and slice thin. Clean peppers and cut small. Melt butter in a large heavy saucepan or soup kettle. Add chopped onions and peppers and cook over a moderate flame until soft. Drain tomatoes, reserve juice, and cut tomatoes into coarse dice. Make bouquet garni. Cut chicken into bite-sized pieces and ham into half-inch squares. Add chicken stock to saucepan or soup kettle. Put in tomato juice, chopped tomatoes, bouquet garni, chopped chicken, ham squares, cayenne pepper, Worcestershire sauce, lima beans, and corn kernels. Simmer, not too gently, for thirty minutes. Taste, correct seasoning with salt and pepper as needed. Heat thoroughly, remove bouquet garni, and serve very hot.

II. Texas Billie's Brunswick Stew (*Traditional Version*)

(*Serves* 6)

2 large onions
½ pound lean ham, about ¼ inch thick
2 squirrels, skinned, cleaned, and cut up
4 medium tomatoes
2 red peppers
1 green pepper
6 ears corn
bouquet garni (G)
(6 sprigs parsley
½ teaspoon thyme
12 peppercorns)
1 pint lima beans
½ teaspoon cayenne pepper
4 tablespoons Worcestershire sauce
1 teaspoon salt
½ teaspoon freshly ground black pepper
2 tablespoons filé gumbo

Slice the onions thin. Remove fat from ham and cut the ham into half-inch squares. Put onion, ham, and cut-up squirrels into a large saucepan or soup kettle, add two quarts water, and simmer one hour. While the contents of the saucepan are simmering, skin the tomatoes and cut into three-quarter-inch pieces. Clean the red and green peppers, and chop approximately the same size as the tomatoes. Cut raw corn off cob. Make bouquet garni. At the end of the first hour, add: the chopped tomatoes, peppers, corn, bouquet garni, lima beans, cayenne pepper. Worcestershire sauce, salt, and pepper. Cover and simmer thirty minutes, skimming soup as required. Take pot from fire, and remove squirrel pieces. Bone squirrel, discarding bones, and return squirrel meat to saucepan. Simmer another thirty minutes. Discard bouquet garni, taste, correct seasoning—you will probably want to add salt. Remove saucepan from fire and stir in the filé gumbo. Mix well and let stand over very low heat five minutes. Under no circumstances allow the soup to come to a boil after the filé gumbo has been added. Should it be necessary to reheat the soup later, use a double boiler. To boil or even simmer soup with filé gumbo in it will make the soup stringy. Serve very hot.

SUGGESTED MENU

Whether or not Texas Billie is right about the origin of Brunswick Stew, it is a distinctly American dish, and should be accompanied by a distinctly American bread, which in this case is corn sticks. Hazel's Herbage (G) falls in the same category and makes an excellent follow-up to any stew as rich as this one. On the same principle, the wine should likewise, I am sure, be native to the United States. Louis Martini's mountain red would do exceeding well.

OFF-AND-ON-HAND SOUP

(*Serves 4*)

The name is curious but apt. The soup can be made in an offhand way from the contents of any well-stocked larder with on-hand ingredients. The only exception to "On-Handness" might be beef stock, but if Campbell's Beef broth is substituted for the homemade variety, everything should be available without a trip to the local grocery store. The soup is a good luncheon when an unexpected guest arrives, or when no plans have been made for lunch or supper but hunger suddenly rears its ugly head. It is a two-martini-on-the-rocks-with-a-twist dish, unless the drinks are gulped. The actual cooking time is forty minutes or less. Add another ten for preparation, a further ten to make a salad, and the meal is ready to eat in an hour. The wine should be chilling before the soup is started. Because the dish is designed for informal meals, its preparation can be expedited by inviting the guests into the kitchen to have their drinks. Once there, they are trapped, and can be utilized for such fiddling jobs as chopping onions, peeling garlic, dicing a green pepper or a carrot. Executive planning in allotting the chores can appreciably reduce the time necessary to get the meal on the table. Any sharp yellow cheese may be substituted for Cheddar.

1 large onion
½ green pepper
3 large stalks celery
1 carrot
4 tablespoons butter
4 tablespoons flour
1 teaspoon dry mustard
1 tablespoon Worcestershire sauce
1 large clove garlic
½ teaspoon monosodium glutamate
2 cups beef stock
6 ounces Cheddar cheese
24 cocktail frankfurters
1 quart milk
1 teaspoon salt
½ teaspoon freshly ground pepper
6 dashes Tabasco

Peel and chop onion, clean and dice green pepper, dice celery to make one cup, scrape and dice carrot. Melt butter in a large saucepan or soup kettle, add onion and celery. Cook, stirring occasionally with a wooden spoon, over a moderate flame for about ten minutes. Add flour, and make a roux (G), cooking for about five minutes. Put in carrot, green pepper, dry mustard, and Worcestershire sauce. Add garlic, through a press or minced. Add monosodium glutamate, blend well, and pour in beef stock. Bring to a boil, cover, and simmer for fifteen minutes. While pot is a-simmer, shred or grind the cheese, and cut the frankfurters into very thin slices. When the soup has simmered fiteen minutes, put in the milk, bring almost to a boil, add cheese, stir continuously until cheese has melted. Add salt, pepper, and Tabasco. Stir well and taste. Correct seasoning—the soup should be highly flavored. Add frankfurter slices. Bring soup to a simmer again. It is now ready to serve.

SUGGESTED MENU

Cheese and crackers are a well-known American combination. Crackers of almost any kind enhance this soup. Crackers also go well with a mixed green salad ennobled with a few chunks of avocado. The salad should follow the soup. The red wine of Burgundy is usually drunk with cheese by gourmets, but this soup really calls for a white wine. A Pouilly Fumé would be a good compromise.

III

EUROPE

CREAM OF LEEK

(*Serves 4*)

The leek is one of the oldest-known cultivated vegetables. It was grown in Cleopatra's Egypt, whence it was probably brought to Rome by returning legionaries, possibly even great Julius himself. Nero, the famous violin virtuoso and alleged arsonist, ate leeks regularly to clear his voice for singing. Good as they are, however, it is unlikely that leeks contributed anything to that Caesar's many and divers talents. Meanwhile, apparently, other Roman legions had brought cultivated leeks to Britain. Centuries later, because of a Welsh soldier—a certain Captain Fluellen—the leek became one of the most famous vegetables in English literature thanks to Shakespeare's *King Henry V*. Why Ancient Pistol so disliked leeks, even raw, has always been a mystery to gourmets. Eating the soup will not solve the mystery but will delight the taste buds, vanquish hunger, and fortify the body.

The length of time required to make this soup depends on whether your Béchamel Sauce is already made or whether you have to make it. If it is already made, the soup will take about forty-five minutes. If you have to make the sauce, it should be your first chore. The total time will be determined by your skill in making sauces.

1 pound fresh leeks
4 tablespoons butter
1 cup chicken stock
4 cups Béchamel Sauce (G)
1 cup cream
1 tablespoon minced chervil (fresh or dried)

Wash the leeks and cut into two-inch lengths, including about half of the green tops. Shred them. Meanwhile, bring two quarts water to a boil in a saucepan. Throw in the shredded leeks and blanch for three minutes. Drain. Melt the butter in a large, heavy saucepan, put in the leeks, and add the chicken stock. Stir well, cover, and simmer for fifteen minutes, stirring to avoid scorching. Slowly stir in Béchamel Sauce. Pour the mixture into a blender, and blend at high speed for forty-five seconds. Return to the saucepan and keep warm. Immediately before serving, bring to a boil, remove from fire and add cream. (If the soup is too thick for your taste, add a little milk.) Mix well and pour into hot soup plates. Sprinkle each plate with some chervil, and serve.

SUGGESTED MENU

Salads with cream soups should avoid mayonnaise. So, taking one consideration with another, salad and bread from Ireland would be a happy solution. Serve Old Man Sean's Sallet (G), and Brigid's Bread (G). Wines are not too appropriate with cream soups, but if it is a gala occasion or something is to be gained through alcohol, remember that champagne can be served with anything, or nothing, for that matter.

A SHAVIAN CUCUMBER SOUP

(*Serves 4*)

Any connection between G.B.S. and this magnificent cold summer soup is, as writers of fiction say, purely coincidental. The recipe comes from another person of the same surname who has as valid a claim to its adjectival rendering as did the witty, wild Irishman. More claim, in the context of a recipe book. G. B. Shaw was a vegetarian; A. Shaw, a friend of mine, not only enjoys fine food of whatever source but also cooks it superbly. Good cold soups are few and it is meet and proper that the source of this one be recognized by name. The cook for whom this recognition and thanks are intended will understand. Most others, while enjoying the dish, may wonder who A. Shaw is and ruminate on the great gustatory debt they incur by eating it.

One word of caution; if you or your guests do not like or are allergic to cucumbers, eschew the Shavian soup. It is loaded. The cucumbers should be integrated with the rest of the soup at the last minute or they lose their crispness, and the dish, much of its felicity.

This soup can be prepared in twenty minutes. The only time factor involved is that required for chilling, which should be about three hours in a normal refrigerator. If a soup is to be served at lunch, a 9 o'clock start in the kitchen will have you out by 9:20 and the soup in the refrigerator waiting for luncheon. It is suggested below that smoked salmon be served with the soup. Preparing the salmon will require as much time as preparing the soup.

6 scallions
1½ pints plain yogurt
½ tablespoon salt
1 teaspoon freshly ground white pepper
1 pint cold milk
⅛ teaspoon cayenne pepper
3 large cucumbers
paprika

Mince the scallions very fine, using about half the green tops as well as the white bottoms. Place the yogurt in a chilled bowl. Add the salt, the minced scallions, the white pepper, and the milk. Stir all very well. Add the cayenne, and stir once more. Place the bowl, covered, in the refrigerator to cool. It should stand at least three hours. Peel the skin off the cucumbers. Cut each in half lengthwise and cut all the white part off around the seed core. Discard the cores, and dice the cucumber meat very small, not more than a quarter of an inch. Place that in another bowl, and refrigerate it. When ready to serve, mix thoroughly the contents of the two bowls, sprinkle lightly with paprika, and put on the table at once.

SUGGESTED MENU

Cucumbers and salmon, fresh or smoked, have an enormous affinity. Instead of a salad, therefore, serve thin slices of cold poached fresh salmon or smoked Scotch salmon with the soup. Scotch salmon is truly smoked; most cured salmon in the United States is salted and is not appropriate with this dish. A lemon wedge and a few capers should accompany the salmon, which in turn should rest gaily on shreds of crisp green lettuce. Slightly toasted and hot saltines are an excellent accompaniment. Hot, freshly made Melba toast would be equally good. A very light, very dry, and well-chilled white wine, such as a Soave or one of the more tender Rieslings would add to the meal.

MOCK TURTLE

(*Serves 4*)

"The only thing better than turtle soup," White Rabbit's last Duchess might have said, "is mock turtle soup. And the moral of that is: When the voice of the mock turtle is heard in the land it may be the mee of a calf." Obviously Sir John Tenniel was aware of what underlay this adage. His famous depiction of the mock turtle leaves no room for doubt. Neither Sir John nor the Reverend Charles Dodgson was noted for his culinary skill, but then either or both probably had access to Mrs. Beeton's *Household Management*. Alice, it would seem, showed remarkable sensitivity for a child in not asking the weeping mock turtle for the recipe for the soo-oop about which he sang so be-ootifully and so dolefully. A somewhat older but no less attractive girl once stated she wanted to make Mock Turtle Soup, but did not know where to get a mock turtle. It was a little like the twelfth grader who had been reading Scott and who asked his teacher: "What kind of a bush is an am?"

The proper construction of the Duchess's traditional Mock Turtle Soup, of which she was so inordinately fond, is really a complex, protracted, and rather grisly operation. A reasonably good facsimile, however, can be produced in about an hour. The result is a kind of Mock Mock Turtle Soup. In simple English this means using two kinds of real turtle soup and some other ingredients. The result looks and tastes like Mock Turtle Soup. Some there be, 'tis said, who do not like Mock Turtle Soup. They may like the first version. Those who wish to serve the kind of Mock Turtle Soup eulogized by Lewis Carroll will find it in the second recipe.

One of the problems in making proper Mock Turtle Soup is what to do with the calf's teeth. They seem almost too pretty to throw away. Perhaps they should be drilled, strung on a silk thread, and presented to the guest of honor as a necklace. If a shark's tooth necklace, why not a mock turtle's tooth necklace?

I. Mock Turtle Soup (*Quick Version*)

(*Serves 4*)

3 cans Campbell's frozen Snapper Turtle Soup (10 oz. each)
½ pound lean veal
2 tablespoons butter
2 medium carrots
1 medium-large turnip
1 can Ancora Green Turtle Soup (20 oz.)
½ cup dry sherry
2 hard-cooked eggs
salt
pepper

Thaw snapper soup according to directions on the cans. Remove all fat and gristle from the veal and cut meat into half-inch cubes. Put butter in a skillet and brown veal quickly on all sides over a medium-hot flame. Drain veal cubes. Scrape carrots, peel turnip and chop into small dice. Drain Ancora Green Turtle Soup, discarding the turtle meat. (To throw it away would be a fault; put it in refrigerator and use it next time you serve green turtle soup.) Place Green Turtle Soup in top half of a large double boiler. Add veal cubes and diced vegetables. Cover and simmer over direct heat, not gently, for fifteen or twenty minutes, or until veal is cooked through. Add thawed Snapper Soup. Stir well. Place over hot water in a double boiler, add sherry, stir again, and heat thoroughly. Meanwhile, slice eggs thin. When soup is hot, taste, and correct seasoning with salt, pepper, or additional sherry. When ready to serve, garnish with egg slices.

II. Mock Turtle Soup (*Traditional Version*)

(*Serves 4*)

1 calf's head
1 veal knuckle, about three pounds
1 marrow bone, about one pound
3 medium carrots
2 medium onions
2 eggs
bouquet garni (G)
 (1 teaspoon thyme
 1 teaspoon marjoram
 1 bay leaf
 8 whole cloves
 18 peppercorns
 ½ teaspoon celery seed
 1 teaspoon allspice
 ½ teaspoon mace)
1 medium turnip
2 tablespoons butter
3 tablespoons flour
2 tablespoons lemon juice
½ cup dry sherry
salt
pepper

Have the butcher remove and retain the eyes and brains of the calf's head. Have him also remove the tongue, and split the head into four equal pieces. Put the pieces, the tongue, the veal knuckle, and marrow bone into a large soup kettle and cover with four and a half quarts cold water. Bring slowly to a boil, cover, and simmer for two hours. While pot is simmering, prepare the other ingredients. Scrape one carrot and cut it into one-inch chunks. Peel the onions and slice them. Hard-cook the eggs and place in refrigerator to cool. Make bouquet garni. Peel and dice the turnip. Scrape and dice the remaining carrots. When the kettle has simmered two hours, remove meat and bones, and allow broth and bones to cool in separate bowls. When bones are cool enough to handle put broth in refrigerator, and remove meat from bones. Cut meat from cheeks of calf, and any meat from veal knuckle, into half-inch cubes, and reserve. Chop all other meat, including tongue, after skinning it, into large pieces and put through a meat chopper using coarse blade. Skim off and discard all fat from broth. Return to kettle, add carrot chunks, onion slices, bouquet garni, and meat that has been through chopper. Cover kettle and simmer one hour and a half. Meanwhile, shell eggs and cut into thin slices. Place butter in a saucepan, melt, and add flour to make a roux (G). Cook it slowly, stirring frequently, to brown it. Add to roux about one and a half cups of hot strained broth and make a thick sauce. When kettle has simmered the required time, strain remaining broth through a kitchen sieve, and return to kettle, discarding contents of sieve. Add to kettle: diced carrot and turnip, and reserved cubed meat, lemon juice, sherry, and sauce. Stir very hard until sauce is integral to the soup. Taste, and correct seasoning with salt and pepper. When soup has simmered twenty-five minutes, add egg slices and simmer five minutes more. Soup is ready to be served. Properly made the soup should not be so thick as a bisque or so thin as a consommé but 'twill serve.

SUGGESTED MENU

Brigid's Bread (G) is a good accompaniment to the soup. Old Man Sean's Sallet (G) would add something to this luncheon as would a bottle of the red wine of Bordeaux, or "claret" as Lewis Carroll would have called it.

OXTAIL SOUP

(*Serves 4*)

Although Oxtail Soup is made in many lands, this version is adapted from an English recipe, originally intended to nourish invalids. For healthy adults, temporarily in an invalid status induced by overeating at a previous meal or overdrinking at any time, it serves a laudable purpose. A number of sworn testimonials to that effect are at hand, including one of my own. Peterkin Pepit almost always had it available. It is said that he occasionally ate it for breakfast. Its use, however, need not be limited by its therapeutic value, as Oxtail Soup makes an excellent luncheon or supper. It may be used, too, as a light soup at dinner. When so served, the quantity of carrots, turnips, and ham should be reduced by about 60 percent. This recipe is based on canned, concentrated Oxtail Soup, each can containing approximately ten ounces. The commercial product tested was that of S. S. Pierce in Boston, although there are probably other brands which will serve as well.

For those who wish to try their hand at the traditional version, which is what Pepit insisted on—he had an excellent chef—recipe II is recommended. It is well to have the butcher cut the tail into sections at the joints.

I. Oxtail Soup (*Quick Version*)

(*Serves 4*)

- 2 medium turnips
- 4 cans concentrated oxtail soup (10 oz. each)
- 4 cups chicken stock
- 2 ounces vermicelli
- 2 slices lean cooked ham, about ¼ inch thick
- Scotch Bonnet (G)

Peel turnips and cut into quarter-inch dice. Place soup in a saucepan. Add chicken stock, put in diced turnips, cover, and simmer briskly for twenty minutes over a low flame, stirring now and again. While soup simmers, break the vermicelli into two-inch lengths, and cut ham into quarter-inch cubes. At the end of twenty minutes' simmering, add the vermicelli and continue to simmer another five minutes. Put in ham, add six dashes Scotch Bonnet, and simmer until soup is hot through. It is now ready to serve. It may be kept hot in a double boiler until needed, but should not be cooked any longer.

II. Oxtail Soup (*Traditional Version*)

(*Serves 4*)

- 1 large oxtail
- 1 medium onion
- 3 tablespoons butter
- 8 whole cloves
- 2 celery tops
- 1 teaspoon salt
- 1 teaspoon black pepper
- 2 large carrots
- 2 medium turnips
- 2 slices lean cooked ham, about ¼ inch thick
- 2 ounces vermicelli
- Scotch Bonnet (G)

Cut oxtail at joints and remove all fat possible. Plunge oxtail into rapidly boiling, slightly salted water and blanch for five minutes. Meanwhile peel and quarter the onion. Drain oxtail, put butter in a skillet, and cook the oxtail sections until brown on all sides. Discard butter and transfer oxtail to a large, heavy saucepan or soup kettle. Pour in three pints water, add onion, cloves, celery tops, salt, and pepper. Bring to a boil, remove any scum, reduce heat, cover, and simmer for four hours. Skim from time to time as necessary. Strain, reserving both broth and oxtail. Place in separate containers and allow to cool. As soon as oxtail is cool enough to handle comfortably, remove from bones and reserve all edible lean meat, discarding bones, skin, and gristle. While broth is cooling, peel carrots and turnips and chop into small dice to make a cup and a half each. Dice ham, and break vermicelli into two-inch pieces. When broth is cold (refrigeration will speed the cooling process), clean and discard all fat from the top. Return cleansed broth to the kettle. Bring to a boil, add reserved ox meat, diced carrots and turnips, and vermicelli. Cover and simmer about ten minutes. Add diced ham and three dashes Scotch Bonnet. Simmer another five minutes or until carrots and turnips are done. The soup is now ready to serve. If a thicker broth is desired, mix a generous tablespoon arrowroot flour with three tablespoons cold broth to make a thin paste, add to the soup just as it begins to boil, and stir well. Simmer briefly after adding paste.

SUGGESTED MENU

Rather than a salad, serve before the soup portions of smoked Scotch salmon. Place a few crisp lettuce leaves on each of four plates, arrange two almost transparent but generous slices of salmon per person on the lettuce. Accompany the salmon by a communal bowl of minced scallions, one of capers, a cruet of olive oil, a small pitcher of lemon juice, and a pepper grinder containing Java peppercorns. With the salmon and the soup serve thin slices of pumpernickel or unsalted crackers—biscuits, to English readers. Selection of a wine poses a problem. Although nourishing, the broth is thin and would not support anything but a very light wine. Many years ago the English came to know the red wine of Bordeaux as "claret." A very light claret, then, if wine at all.

IRISH BROTH JOHN L. SULLIVAN

(*Serves 4*)

This is obviously what the Irish mean when they speak of "a broth of a boy." Anyone but the Irish would call this a heavy soup, or perhaps even a stew. It is probably the very one indeed that John L. Sullivan, "the strong boy of Boston," ate on that July day when he broke all the ribs of Jake Kilrain. Kilrain should have eaten some too. This broth is also a little reminiscent of the stew mentioned in "An Irish Ballad" by that mathematical genius and wandering minstrel from Harvard, Tom Lehrer, who had a vogue as a balladeer in the middle fifties. In the present instance, however, you omit the baby brother, although you may certainly invite the neighbors in. They will be grateful. This is indeed and all a fine broth of a soup.

The dish takes about two and a half hours to prepare. It may be eaten at once or left standing in the pot, covered, for twenty-four hours, even in moderately warm weather (75°), when it can be refrigerated and will keep another two days. If not eaten at once, it may thicken and require additional water. Before adding water, bring the soup to a boil. If still too thick, gradually thin with water. This recipe will make an adequate lunch or supper for four unless all are very hungry. A similar but not so hearty soup may be put together in about fifteen minutes by using two canned soups. This quickie belongs in the middleweight, not the heavyweight division.

I. Irish Broth John L. Sullivan (*Quick Version*)

(*Serves 4*)

2 cans Scotch Broth (10 oz. each)
2 cans Cock-a-Leekie Soup (10 oz. each)

Combine the contents of the cans in the top of a double boiler or in a saucepan. If you use the latter, the soup must be stirred frequently to prevent scorching; if cooked over water, stirring is unnecessary except at the moment of serving. When the soup is heated through, add hot water if it is too thick, and serve at once in hot soup plates.

Moving up into the heavyweight division, John L. Sullivan's broth is prepared in about thirty rounds under Marquis of Queensberry rules. It ends in a knockout.

II. Irish Broth John L. Sullivan (*Traditional Version*)

(*Serves 4*)

2 pounds shin of beef
salt
pepper
6 tablespoons barley
1 medium carrot
1 small turnip
1 small onion
1 large stalk celery
2 medium leeks
3 tablespoons minced parsley
3 tablespoons butter

Cut the meat from the bone, remove and discard as much fat and gristle as possible. Chop the meat into half-inch cubes. Place the meat and the bone in a large, heavy soup kettle. Add about a tablespoon salt and half as much pepper. Pour in seven cups of water, cover the kettle, and bring to a boil over a high flame. Add barley, lower flame, and simmer, covered. In half an hour skim off scum if necessary. Allow soup to simmer a total of an hour and a half, skimming as required. While the soup is a-simmer—a crossword puzzle word—scrape and dice the carrot and turnip. Peel the onion, dice it and celery, and chop the leeks, including most of the green, into quarter-inch slices. Mince the parsley. After the soup has simmered for an hour and a quarter, melt the butter in a large skillet and add all the chopped vegetables except the parsley. Cook over a moderate fire for five or six minutes. When your watch or timer announces the end of that hour and a half, add the contents of the skillet to the broth and continue to simmer for another ten minutes. Correct the seasoning; it will probably need salt. Add parsley and the broth is ready. Serve in large, hot soup plates.

SUGGESTED MENU

Because of the heartiness of the main dish, a light salad is indicated. It should be Irish. What could be better than Old Man Sean's Sallet (G) to be sure? Brigid's Bread (G) is the obvious choice in that department, although you may want no bread at all. If you must have wine, make it a good table type, robust and red. John L. Sullivan took whiskey.

SOPA DE CAMARÃO E LAGOSTA
(Shrimp and Lobster Soup)
(Serves 4)

One of the small extra vacations which Peterkin Pepit allowed himself was an occasional trip to Portugal, primarily for the purpose of drinking white port in its own habitat. That eminent tosspot was excessively fond of the drink's golden smoothness and would spend many hours in Lisbon sipping it at the Rex Bar, which has, no doubt, long since disappeared. One evening, dining at home with our mutual friend Dr. Dottle, he extolled the merits of white port to such effect that the orthopedist agreed to accompany Pepit on his next trip. The two men did not confine themselves to drinking port but managed to find time to consume food native to the country. Among the dishes which they both enjoyed was a fine, filling soup known as Sopa de Camarão. Dottle felt that it might be improved by the inclusion of a small quantity of crayfish. It is his recipe that follows.

1 carrot
1 celery stalk with leaves
3 sprigs parsley
1 pound medium green shrimp
1 rock lobster (approximately 8 oz.)
1 large onion
4 tablespoons butter
4 tablespoons flour
1 cup dry white wine
salt
pepper
small croutons (G)

Scrape carrot; chop it and celery into quarters. Put two quarts water in a large saucepan. Add the carrot, celery, and parsley. Bring to a boil. Put in shrimp and lobster tail. Cover, and simmer not too gently for about six minutes. Remove shrimp and continue simmering the lobster tail for another ten minutes. Drain, reserving liquid. While saucepan simmers, peel and cut the onion very small. Place butter in another heavy saucepan and cook the onion over low heat until it is golden. Stir frequently to prevent burning. Add flour and make a roux (G). Allow roux to cook about five minutes. As soon as lobster tail is cool enough to handle—it may be cooled under running cold water—remove meat from shell and chop fine. Clean shrimp and set eight aside. Chop the remainder small. Gradually add three pints of the reserved liquid to the roux, stirring with a wooden spoon over a low heat to make a slightly thick soup. Put in the chopped lobster and shrimp. Add the wine. Season with salt and pepper to taste. Place contents of saucepan in a blender and blend at high speed for thirty seconds. Return soup to saucepan. Heat gently until hot through. Garnish with reserved shrimp. The soup is ready to serve.

SUGGESTED MENU

Place a bowl of small croutons (G) beside each diner to nibble on or put in the soup as he sees fit. No other bread is indicated. Hazel's Herbage (G) would make a becoming salad. For wine, a Portuguese vintage known as Casal Garcia is excellent with the soup.

QUARTER-OF-AN-HOUR SOUP

(*Serves 4*)

The well-known theory that Spaniards have no regard for time is a canard of the finest feather. They know so well how to use time that they sensibly close everything up at midday in order to enjoy a leisurely lunch and a siesta. Time has few better uses. At the end of the day, they do not rush madly home or to a restaurant for dinner. That ruins the digestion and the temper. No Spaniard would think of eating dinner before ten o'clock; even that is considered early. It is, therefore, a little difficult to account for the name of this soup, which requires considerably more than a quarter of an hour to make or to eat. The cook who named it may have had a faulty kitchen timer; more likely he had no clock at all. Sometimes two hours seem to pass in fifteen minutes; other times fifteen minutes seem to last two hours. Whatever the origin of the name, the soup makes a delicious and filling meal.

The original Spanish recipe is, in my opinion, more rewarding and it can be prepared in about two hours if you work rapidly. Only if you are in a hurry and particularly want to serve Quarter-of-an-Hour Soup, should you make it as in I. The extra time required by II will whet the appetite and give your guests an opportunity to wet their respective whistles.

The two hours usually required to make the soup can be cut in half by using the following version:

I. Quarter-of-an-Hour Soup (*Quick Version*)

(*Serves 4*)

12 raw shrimp
6 scallions
½ cup blanched almonds
½ pound sliced lean cooked ham about ¼ inch thick
2 tablespoons olive oil
2 cans Underwood minced clams (5½ oz. each)
1½ cups cooked rice
2 tablespoons tomato paste
3 cups chicken stock
3 tablespoons dry sherry
⅓ cup cooked peas
6 dashes Scotch Bonnet (G)

Peel the shrimp and cut into half-inch pieces. Chop the scallions fine. Grind the almonds in a Mouli grater. Cut ham into half-inch pieces. Place the olive oil in a heavy saucepan or soup kettle. Heat, add scallions, and cook over a moderate flame until soft, about ten minutes. Meanwhile, strain the clams, reserving both the clams and the juice. When scallions are cooked, add the shrimp, almonds, and ham to the saucepan. Mix ingredients well and cook, stirring frequently, until shrimp are pink. This will take about five minutes. Between stirrings, wash rice well, and mix tomato paste with four tablespoons water. Pour in the chicken stock, and the reserved clam juice. Add tomato paste mixture, rice, and the sherry. Bring to a boil; simmer for ten minutes more. Add the peas, the minced clams, and the Scotch Bonnet. Cook until hot through and serve.

II. Quarter-of-an-Hour Soup (*Traditional Version*)

(*Serves* 4)

1 pint shucked clams and juice	½ cup blanched almonds
2 eggs	1½ tablespoons olive oil
1 large tomato	3 cups chicken stock
1 onion	½ cup uncooked rice
3 slices ham, ¼ inch thick	⅓ cup green peas
12 large green shrimp	1½ tablespoons sherry

Place clams and juice in a saucepan, bring rapidly to a boil, and immediately remove from fire. Drain clams, reserving both juice and clams. Hard-cook eggs. While eggs are cooking, remove and discard the feet of the clams (see Clam Chowder Miles Standish, p. 20) and cut the remainder coarsely. When eggs are done, mince and set aside. Immerse the tomato in boiling water for thirty seconds, skin, and dice coarsely. Peel and chop onion fine; dice ham. Shell shrimp. Grind almonds in a Mouli grater. Place olive oil in a large saucepan, and cook onion until tender. Push the onion aside; add shrimp, ham, and almonds. Cook, stirring constantly without disturbing onions, until shrimp are pink all over. Remove shrimp from saucepan and chop fine; add clam juice and stock to saucepan. Wash rice thoroughly in cold water. Bring mixture in saucepan to a boil, put in rice, tomato, and minced eggs. Stir well. Cover, and reduce heat; simmer ten minutes. Add peas and sherry, and continue to simmer another twenty minutes. Add chopped shrimp and clams, stir well, simmer about five minutes until hot through, and serve in hot soup plates.

SUGGESTED MENU

Light, thick-crusted Spanish bread should be served with the soup. French bread is a good substitute if Spanish bread is not available. Spain grows some of the world's best oranges so that Hazel's Herbage (G) would be an appropriate salad. Logroño in northern Spain produces several varieties of pleasant, light, dry white wine. One is Las Veras. It is available in the United States at very modest prices. Try it with this soup.

LA FRUTA DEL MAR SIETE PUERTAS
(Seafood Soup at the Seven Doors Restaurant)

(*Serves* 6)

Time was when Barcelona was reputed to be the wickedest city in the world, whatever that means. No one was ever turned into a pillar of salt for looking back at it. It has another reputation: its chefs invent and prepare some of the finest seafood dishes in the world. Barcelona's sinister reputation is being challenged, and with appreciable success, by a number of other cities, some of which are no great distance from where this is being written. The Catalan seaport's reputation as a haven for gastronomes is in no danger. No cloud, not even one no bigger than a man's hand, hangs over its restaurants and kitchens. On the Barcelona waterfront, hard by the Columbus Column, is the Seven Doors. Here all the food is excellent—witness the roast leg of baby lamb, one leg to a person —and the seafood is superb. Among the many items offered on the menu is a "Fisherman's Soup" in which are combined fish, crayfish, scallops, shrimp, and probably octopus. The recipe is not included on the menu, and efforts to persuade Barcelona chefs to divulge their secrets are usually met with a complete inability to speak or understand any language but the purest Catalan.

This recipe for a seafood soup is based on what taste, smell, and sight indicated were the ingredients of the Sopa Pescadores. I have omitted octopus as it is difficult to find in the United States. I do not know which Mediterranean fish was used. There may have been two kinds. I have used flounder because it is a white fish, almost always available in fillets. Any other white fish could be used. If you want to try two kinds of fish, I suggest adding bluefish. In that case, of course, you will need only half a pound of flounder and the same amount of bluefish. If bay scallops are not available, substitute deep-sea scallops, and cut them into three-quarter-inch cubes. However you do it, this is a very rich dish. The recipe amply provides for six people.

By reading the recipe carefully and having all the ingredients at hand, one can prepare this soup in an hour of concentrated effort —working like mad.

1 large carrot
2 stalks celery
1 medium onion
1 large leek, white part only
½ cup olive oil
bouquet garni (G)
  (6 sprigs parsley
  1 clove garlic
  12 white peppercorns
  1 bay leaf)
1 pound flounder fillets
5 tablespoons sifted flour
1 scant tablespoon curry powder
3 cups white wine
1 pound spiny lobster tails
¾ pound green shrimp
1 pint bay scallops
12 tablespoons barely cooked rice
4 ounces whipping cream
2 teaspoons shredded saffron
salt
freshly ground white pepper
fresh chives

Scrape the carrot and cut into moderate dice. Chop the celery into similar pieces. Peel the onion and chop it fine. Wash the leek thoroughly and cut to match the onion. Put olive oil into a soup kettle or large saucepan. Heat oil, add chopped vegetables, and cook over a moderate flame until onion is soft, stirring from time to time. While vegetables are cooking make the bouquet garni. Chop the flounder into one-inch squares. By now the onion should be cooked. Mix the flour and curry powder in a small bowl. Add to the contents of the saucepan, and make a roux (G). Stir and cook for about five minutes, until roux is done and well combined with the vegetables. Gradually add the wine and two cups water, stirring until the mixture is smooth. Put in the bouquet garni, the fish, and the lobster tails. Cover and simmer about fifteen minutes. Now add the green shrimp, scallops, and cooked rice. Cover and simmer three minutes. Take soup off fire. Remove lobster tails and green shrimp. Remove and discard shells. Cut shrimp and lobster meat into bite-size pieces, and return to the saucepan. Place soup on fire, and simmer another two minutes. When soup is done, remove bouquet garni, stir in cream, and add saffron. Mix well over low heat with a wooden spoon until soup is a pleasing yellow color. Taste and correct the seasoning with salt and pepper. The soup should be eaten very hot and at once. Soup made with seafood tends to get gummy if allowed to stand, or if reheated, even in a double boiler. Garnish each plate with a goodly quantity of chopped fresh chives.

SUGGESTED MENU

King Cole Slaw (G) goes well with any seafood or fish combination. This one is no exception. Spanish or French bread is a must. The wine should be Spanish, and white, and dry. One of the Riojas —bought from a reliable wine merchant—would be best.

SOPA REAL
(Royal Soup)
(*Serves* 4)

A truly regal dish, normally used in Spain as an opening course at a luncheon or dinner, Sopa Real is here fortified to serve as the principal item on a lunch or supper menu. After one of his periodic visits to Mojacar, a Spanish hill town, Peterkin Pepit wrote in his diary: "If Spain had done nothing else for the world except produce Velásquez, Cervantes, and Sopa Real, it would have done enough." This may be an exaggeration, but not a great one. Properly put together, this is a soup for a king; or for a queen for that matter, particularly if she is being courted.

If you wish to serve it as a separate course rather than as the main dish, omit the beef, and cut the amount of ham and chicken by a half, and the quantity of liquid by one third. Serve it in bouillon cups and garnish each with half a teaspoon of minced parsley. When making it for a soup course, the first, or shorter recipe is recommended.

This is one of those soups mentioned in the introduction where the faster method of preparation yields a result which is as good as, if not better than, making the soup from scratch. In either case eschew the use of grated cheese lest it mask the delicacy of the soup itself. Sopa Real is a superb dish in warm weather because it is light but filling and nourishing. Despite the aristocratic title, the recipe can be made with leftovers if enough of each is available. The local delicatessen can provide already cooked meats as well as canned beef stock. If ingredients are on hand, this soup takes only about twenty minutes to put together.

Despite the fact that making the soup from scratch is to my mind unnecessary, method II is provided for those who believe that soups made in the traditional way are always better than those made by using short cuts.

I. Sopa Real (*Quick Version*)

(*Serves 4*)

2 hard-cooked eggs
3 slices cooked chicken breast
3 slices cooked ham, one quarter inch thick
3 slices well-done roast beef, one quarter inch thick
2 quarts beef stock
¾ cup dry sherry
4 sprigs watercress

Chop eggs, chicken, ham, beef, into quarter-inch dice. Place all in the top of a double boiler, add two quarts of beef stock and sherry, and heat over boiling water until soup is just ready to boil. Serve in hot soup plates, each garnished with a sprig of watercress.

II. Sopa Real (*Traditional Version*)

(*Serves 4*)

2 eggs
2 chicken breasts, boned
3 slices tenderized ham, one quarter inch thick
3 slices lean beef, one quarter inch thick
2 quarts beef stock
¾ cup dry sherry
4 sprigs watercress

Hard-cook the eggs and put in refrigerator to cool. Cut chicken, ham, and beef into quarter-inch dice. Place stock in a heavy saucepan, bring to a boil and add diced meat. Lower flame, cover, and simmer for about forty minutes, or until beef is done. Meanwhile shell eggs and cut into small dice. When beef is done, transfer contents of saucepan to top of double boiler. Add diced eggs and sherry. Cover, and heat over hot water until soup is hot through. Taste, correct seasoning, and serve in hot soup plates, each garnished with a sprig of watercress.

SUGGESTED MENU

The soup may be served with small croutons (G), or with Spanish or French bread, or, indeed, with both. Because it is a comparatively light soup and intended for warm weather, cold cooked artichokes with mayonnaise would make a good salad. A light Spanish table wine called Esmerado is just right with the soup.

SOPA SCIMUNITO AZAFRANADO
(Saffron Noodle Soup)
(*Serves 4*)

A charming and many-talented lady of my acquaintance, who was fortunate enough to live in Spain for a time, kindly provided me with this recipe, which is almost unique among noodle soups. Among her talents are cookery and ceramics, not too bad a combination. One of the advantages to living in Spain is that saffron is comparatively cheap. My friend, who is a lover of both Spanish and Italian food, combined the two. Taking her inexpensive saffron from Spain and her little pasta machine (see Appendix) from Italy —via Sears, Roebuck—she combined saffron and noodles to the greater delectation of her guests.

Noodles may, of course, be made by rolling out the dough with a rolling pin and cutting to size with a knife. This is an arduous and possibly perilous way to make pasta. By far, the easiest and safest way is to use a pasta machine, which can be adjusted to make anything from vermicelli to lasagne. The original recipe, because of the time required to make the noodles, is slow. With my friend's permission, of course, I altered it for the purposes of rapid cooking. The quantities in both the quick (I) and the original (II) recipes are intended for people who really enjoy noodles and only use the soup to moisten them. If you prefer your noodle soup with more liquid, cut down on the noodles or increase the liquid.

I. Sopa Scimunito Azafranado (*Quick Version*)

(*Serves 4*)

1 generous tablespoon saffron
1 teaspoon salt
12 ounces thin noodles
1 small jar cooked chicken
3 cups chicken stock
1 teaspoon freshly ground pepper

Use shredded saffron rather than powdered. Put saffron in a small skillet. Add a half cup of water and simmer gently for fifteen minutes. Fill a large saucepan with water. Add salt. Bring water to a boil. Add noodles and simmer until done. This will probably not be more than ten minutes unless you have a predilection for mush. While noodles are cooking, chop chicken small. Place the stock in a saucepan. Add the contents of the skillet and stir the saffron solution well into the stock. Add freshly ground pepper. Drain noodles. Add them to saucepan and stir well. Add enough water to dilute the soup to your own taste. Correct seasoning.

The original version calls for hard flour (G). Ordinary flour is not up to making proper pasta.

II. Sopa Scimunito Azafranado (*Traditional Version*)

(*Serves 4*)

1 carrot
1 medium onion
1 stalk celery with leaves
2 sprigs parsley
12 peppercorns
1¼ teaspoons salt
8 chicken backs or wings (or a combination)
2 teaspoons saffron
2 eggs
1 egg yolk
1½ cups hard flour
1 teaspoon olive oil
fresh black peppercorns

Place two and a half quarts water in a large saucepan or soup kettle. Bring it to a boil. While water is heating, scrape carrot, peel onion, and cut each into quarters. Cut up celery. Add them, parsley, peppercorns, and one teaspoon of salt. When water has come to a boil, add chicken. Cover and simmer for two hours.

While soup is cooking, prepare the pasta. Place the saffron in a small skillet with half a cup water. Simmer fifteen minutes. Place the contents of skillet, a quarter teaspoon of salt, the eggs, egg yolk, and three-fourths cup of flour into a blender. Blend at high speed for about a minute and a half, being sure to eliminate all lumps. Remove contents of blender to a large bowl and let rest for ten minutes. Add remaining flour and knead into a dough. The dough should be a solid ball. Add olive oil and work in well with your fingers. (In making the dough, of course, you will keep your hands well floured.) Let dough stand for about ten minutes. Meanwhile set up the pasta machine. Shape the dough like a small loaf of French bread and cut off a piece about three inches long, and flatten piece slightly. Sprinkle the pasta machine rollers with flour or place some on the piece of dough and put it through the rollers four times. Decrease the space between rollers each time until you have a long, thin section of dough. Repeat this process with the remaining dough until it is all rolled out flat. Let stand until dry enough to be run through the cutters. This will probably take approximately half an hour, or time for two martinis if you drink fast. Experience alone will tell you when the dough is dry enough. When the dough is ready, sprinkle it with additional flour and run it through the cutters, adjusted to whatever size noodle you want. The noodles should be spread out on paper towels to continue drying until they become brittle. Depending on the humidity, the drying process will take about two hours.

The chicken stock of course will now be done. When it is, remove the chicken and drain the soup into a large bowl, discarding vegetables. Remove all meat from the bones, chop fine, and place in the soup. Discard bones and skin. Remove grease from surface of chicken stock. When noodles are sufficiently dry, fill a large saucepan with water; add noodles, and boil gently ten minutes. Drain noodles; combine with soup. Bring to a boil; add freshly ground pepper to taste, and serve very hot in hot soup plates.

SUGGESTED MENU

Bread hardly seems to be necessary with noodles in this quantity; but a light salad—under the circumstances, this can only be Hazel's Herbage (G)—would make a good accompaniment or a follow-up. For a wine, either Spanish or Italian is indicated. In the latter case, Soave would be a good selection. For a Spanish wine, a light, dry table wine called Blanco Fino would serve well.

GAZPACHO DE SEGOVIA

(*Serves 4*)

Of all the cold soups in the world—there are more than one might believe—Spanish Gazpacho is justly famous and one of the best. When the temperature is above eighty-five degrees Fahrenheit, Gazpacho makes a splendid lunch or supper. It is equally good, in smaller quantities, as a soup course at dinner. Recipes for most provincial dishes vary with the province. Gazpacho is no exception. The kind you eat in Andalucía differs from that in Granada; both are excellent. This recipe, which comes from the area just to the north of Madrid, is representative of all Gazpachos and has the merit of being a little easier to make than some others.

One half hour should be allowed for preparation and three hours for chilling. In some parts of Spain Gazpacho is served with coarse, stale bread crumbs. Put in the soup, they make a kind of mush and detract much, I think, from the crispness inherent to the dish. I once saw a recipe which put Gazpacho through a blender. The resulting purée may be good but is gastronomic heresy. Obviously, some small preparation beforehand will admit of this recipe's being done in about half an hour. If you use already chilled ingredients, you appreciably cut down on the three-hour chilling interval. The items to be chilled are onion, tomatoes, cucumber, green pepper, garlic, lemon juice, tomato juice, and one cup water. As each of the vegetables is chopped, return it to the refrigerator. Store all ingredients in the same bowl. Twenty minutes before serving the soup, add all other items to the bowl, stir and return to the refrigerator for about fifteen minutes. On no account put the olive oil in the refrigerator before adding it to the soup. Regardless of the method employed, the ingredients are the same.

1 large Spanish onion
2 large tomatoes
2 small cucumbers
1 large green pepper
3 cloves garlic
½ teaspoon freshly ground black pepper
1 teaspoon salt
½ teaspoon ground cumin seed
1 teaspoon dry basil (or fresh)
2 tablespoons fresh lemon juice
¼ cup olive oil
2 cups tomato juice
3 dashes Tabasco
2 cups small croutons (G)
4 ice cubes

Peel and chop the onion fine, but do not mince. Place in a large glass bowl. Skin the tomatoes and cucumbers; chop as fine as the onion, and add to the bowl. Remove seeds and membranes from the green pepper, and dice it. Put in bowl. Peel the garlic, put it through a press or mince very fine, and distribute over the other vegetables. Add the freshly ground black pepper, salt, cumin seed, basil, lemon juice, olive oil, tomato juice, 1 cup water, and Tabasco. Cover bowl and put in refrigerator for at least three hours. While soup is chilling, make the croutons. To serve: place an ice cube in each of four soup plates, fill plates with soup, and serve with croutons on the side.

SUGGESTED MENU

Except for wine, Gazpacho is the whole meal. With croutons no bread is needed. The soup is its own salad. A good light, white wine from the north of Spain is Blanco Fino. Properly chilled, it is a pleasant accompaniment to Gazpacho.

DANISH APPLE SOUP

(*Serves 4*)

Soups made from various kinds of fruit are much prized in many parts of the world. Nowhere are they prized more highly than in Scandinavia. The idea of making soups from cherries, various kinds of berries, apples, and other fruits—it has never been established whether a tomato is a fruit or a vegetable—may seem unappetizing to people who have never had the opportunity to eat them. Once you have had such an opportunity, you will understand why fruit soups enjoy such a high reputation. In addition to their taste, they have two recommendations—one, most of them can be made in about an hour; and two, they may be served either hot or cold. If served hot, they should be lightly sprinkled with freshly ground nutmeg. If served cold, they should be garnished with a healthy dollop of whipped cream.

As is apparent from the directions in this book, I find kitchen gadgets efficient and helpful. One of these is a manually operated utensil, an "apple corer and divider." With one stroke you can core an apple and divide it into eight segments. Its use is highly recommended in preparing the following recipe.

3 pounds tart apples
1 large lemon
2 ounces Danish blue cheese
1 cinnamon stick
2 teaspoons salt
½ cup cornstarch
4 pieces zwieback
½ cup dry white wine (Riesling)

Wash, core, but do not peel apples. Cut them into quarters or smaller wedges. Peel lemon and cut peel into narrow strips about an inch long. Juice the lemon. Chop cheese into thin wafers and then cut into small pieces. Place the apples in soup kettle. Add two quarts water. Put in lemon strips and juice. Add the cinnamon stick and the salt. Put in the cheese. Bring to a boil. Cover and boil slowly until apples are very soft, about thirty-five minutes, stirring occasionally. While apples are cooking, place cornstarch in a small bowl. Add one and a half cups water and make a paste. Using a rolling pin or a beer bottle, reduce the zwieback to crumbs. When apples are done, remove and discard cinnamon stick. Put contents of kettle through a blender at high speed for twenty seconds. Return soup to kettle. Add the cornstarch paste and the wine. Cover and simmer slowly until soup thickens to the consistency of cream. Divide the zwieback crumbs among four soup plates. Pour the soup on top of them and serve very hot.

SUGGESTED MENU

The best bread to accompany the soup is Danish rye cut very thin. If this is unavailable, the small slices of "party" rye made in the United States will go well as a substitute. An excellent salad to accompany this particular dish would be a cucumber and endive salad with French dressing (G). The wine, of course, would be Riesling.

DUTCH PEA SOUP

(*Serves 4*)

In tropical climes there are certain times when Dutch pea soup—the Dutch call it *Erwtensoep*—should be avoided. In tropical climes, as a matter of fact, it should be avoided utterly. I attempted it in the middle of a Washington summer, a mistake I am not likely to repeat. The taste was marvelous, but the internal heat generated by the soup seemed to raise the outside temperature from a mere ninety-four degrees Fahrenheit to about a hundred and fifteen. In the normal weather of northern Europe, pea soup makes an excellent lunch or supper; and it is equally good anywhere else, depending on climatic conditions. It would be hard indeed to find any soup better suited to the purposes of this collection of recipes. Erwtensoep has only one drawback: the time required to make it. Those who have eaten it agree that time has few better uses. A partly offsetting advantage is that the soup improves with age and thus may be prepared at least a day before it is needed. It will keep, under refrigeration, for at least a week.

The longer the soup cools the thicker it becomes. If allowed to stand overnight, it can literally be cut with a knife and eaten with a fork. Schools of thought differ on the best consistency of split pea soup. Some like it almost solid; some like it no thicker than light cream. Eat it as it is, or thin to your own liking by gradually adding scalded milk to the hot soup, stirring well as you pour. Both soup and milk must be hot, else you cannot judge the consistency as you dilute.

For those whose mouths have been watering as a result of the deathless prose with which this fine soup is described, but who lack the time to prepare it, a fast version is immediately appended. The traditional Dutch version follows.

I. Dutch Pea Soup (*Quick Version*)

(*Serves 4*)

3 cans frozen Green Pea with Ham Soup (10 oz. each)
4 slices boiled ham, ⅛ inch thick
8 cocktail frankfurters
½ cup sherry
fresh pepper

Thaw soup according to directions on label. While soup is thawing, cut ham into half-inch squares. Slice cocktail frankfurters into half-inch pieces. When soup has thawed, place in top of double boiler, add ham squares, frankfurter slices, and sherry. Place over hot water and heat. When soup is hot through, thin with water to your taste, and sprinkle lightly with freshly ground pepper. Heat until hot through again, and serve.

II. Dutch Pea Soup (*Traditional Version*)

(*Serves 4*)

1 cup split green peas
4 slices bacon
½ pound potatoes
1 small celeriac
½ stalk celery (top half)
1 leek
1 medium onion
3 frankfurters
1 pig's foot
1 pig's ear (optional)
¼ cup sherry
1 tablespoon salt
1 tablespoon fresh pepper

Place three pints water in a soup kettle. Wash peas, add to kettle, and soak for twelve hours. (If you use "quick" peas, soak for two hours.) Bring water to a boil, stir well, reduce heat, cover, and simmer at least two hours. While soup is simmering, cut bacon into squares; peel and slice potatoes thin; scrape and dice celeriac. Chop the celery top. Clean leek and chop into one-inch pieces. Peel onion and chop coarsely. Cut frankfurters into three-quarter-inch pieces. After peas have cooked two hours, add: pig's foot, pig's ear, bacon, potatoes, celeriac, celery tops, leek, and onion. Season with sherry, salt, and pepper. Mix contents of kettle well and continue to simmer, covered, stirring occasionally, for another two and a half hours. Remove and discard pig's foot and ear. Put in the frankfurters and simmer another thirty minutes. The soup is now ready to eat. As indicated, it will be better if allowed to stand overnight on the cold stove. Reheat and serve.

SUGGESTED MENU

Erwtensoep is a very hearty dish and should be followed by a light salad. In view of the soup's origin, Salade Flandre (G) is the obvious choice. For a bread, hard rolls would be a good selection. A good French or American table wine, light and red, would be admirable.

FRENCH ONION SOUP

(*Serves 4*)

When I was nine years old, long before the days of penicillin, I had double pneumonia. The family homeopathic doctor sought to cure me by frequent and repeated application of hot onion plasters to my chest. Theoretically homeopathy teaches that "like cures like." In this instance it was a case, I suspect, of attempting to cure by dislike. The pneumococci presumably disliked the smell of hot onions and departed. At least that is what they were supposed to do. They did not. My life, for good or ill, was saved by other and more conventional means. For many years the sole result of the treatment was to make me recoil at the smell of onions. Even today I shed fluent and bitter tears every time I chop them. Nevertheless, candor compels me to admit that I am extremely fond of onion soup, so that I am willing to shed the tears and take the time necessary to make it.

It seems hardly necessary to point out that French Onion Soup is one of the great peasant soups of that country; indeed of the world. As an acquaintance of mine was wont to say—I never knew why—"you can't go wrong on the neighborhood." Well, you can't go wrong if you serve this soup for a hearty lunch, an informal supper, or, as a bonus after a cocktail party when you and your guests have reason to anticipate the next morning with loathing.

For such an occasion as the last there is a rapid method of making French Onion Soup. Most commercial onion soups are either too thin or too thick. By adding water to thin the condensed variety, you reduce its therapeutic effect. By combining a thick and a thin soup, however, you get the proper consistency and maintain all the desirable qualities. The combination of soups is effected as follows:

I. French Onion Soup (*Quick Version*)

(*Serves* 4)

- 3 cans condensed onion soup (10 oz. each)
- 2 cans uncondensed onion soup (13 oz. each)
- ½ cup dry sherry
- 4 large croutons (G)
- 8 tablespoons grated Parmesan cheese

In a saucepan, combine the soups, add the sherry, and bring slowly to a simmer. Just as the soup begins to boil, place the croutons in the soup plates, pour the soup over them, sprinkle with grated cheese and serve.

II. French Onion Soup (*Traditional Version*)

(*Serves* 4)

- 4 large Spanish onions (about 3 pounds total)
- 3 tablespoons butter
- 2 cloves garlic
- ½ teaspoon pepper
- 2 tablespoons flour
- 1 quart rich beef stock
- 1 cup good Burgundy
- 4 large croutons (G)
- 8 tablespoons grated cheese

Peel and slice the onions into semi-rings. Place the butter in a large, heavy saucepan, melt butter, and add the garlic by putting it through a garlic press. You may, of course, mince the garlic very fine, or mash it. A press is better. When the butter is hot, add the onions and cook over a very high flame, manuevering the onions with a wooden spoon violently and frequently, for fifteen minutes. Reduce heat and sprinkle in the pepper and the flour. Cook slowly, stirring very frequently for five minutes. Pour in the beef stock, cover, and simmer slowly for one hour. Add the Burgundy, stir well, and taste. Correct the seasoning. You may want more salt.

In each of four hot soup plates, place one large crouton, fill the plates with onion soup very hot and sprinkle each with two tablespoons grated cheese. Serve forthwith.

SUGGESTED MENU

Serve no bread, as bread is already in the soup. Because of the soup's basic origin, the wine should be a simple red table wine, but with some body. In this instance a good red Bordeaux should be considered. For salad nothing could be better than a mixed green salad with French dressing. This starts as a French meal and should be kept that way.

RED BEAN SOUP

(Serves 4)

Les Halles, the great Paris market, is being moved from the center of the city to an outlying area. The transfer of the market may be sound economically, aesthetically, and logistically—the traffic problems of Paris are famous—but the effect on the many small bistros and restaurants in the area can only be deplored. Even if Les Halles' renowned onion soup remains available, eating it in the early morning before going home after a night on the town is bound to lose some of its zest. Gone will be the romantic bustle of the market place, the confusion of the arriving trucks with their loads of fresh vegetables, seafood, and graphic odors. Many of the small eating places are unprepossessing from the outside, but most of them serve excellent meals. One of the pleasantest both outside and inside is Pharamond—long may it prosper. There I ate the epitome of Red Bean Soup. It was smooth, rich, and delicious. The following recipe will give you a very close approximation of the flavor and texture. While the soup is basically intended for the main course at lunch or supper, it can be served in small quantities as a first course at dinner.

Preparation of most bean soups requires a bit of time. The judicious combination of canned vegetables, however, permits you to make Red Bean Soup in less than an hour, quick version I. The traditional recipe II takes overnight.

I. Red Bean Soup (*Quick Version*)

(Serves 4)

5 slices bacon
1 small can cooked whole white onions (7½ oz.)
½ can S.S. Pierce baby carrots (16 oz. per can)
2 cans tomatoes (20 oz. each)
2 cans red kidney beans (16 oz. per can)
2 cups whole fresh celery leaves
1 bottle good Burgundy
1 small bunch parsley

Cook bacon in a skillet slowly until crisp. While bacon cooks, drain onions, carrots, tomatoes, and beans, reserving the juice from each. Chop onions and carrots small and the tomatoes coarsely. Mince celery leaves. When bacon is done, drain on paper towels and crumble or chop small. Place all reserved juices in a large saucepan, pour in wine, and add all other ingredients except parsley. Cover saucepan, bring to a boil, reduce heat, and simmer twenty minutes. While soup simmers, mince parsley. At the end of the twenty minutes, remove soup from fire, and allow to cool until it can be put into a blender, about five minutes. Run through the blender at medium speed for twenty seconds. (You will probably have to make several runs because of the quantity.) Put soup through a medium-coarse kitchen strainer, discarding residue in strainer. Return soup to saucepan and heat through. When ready to serve, and it should be very hot, garnish with minced parsley.

II. Red Bean Soup (*Traditional Version*)

(*Serves 4*)

3 cups dry red kidney beans
5 large tomatoes
2 medium carrots
1 large onion
2 cups celery leaves, whole
5 slices bacon
1 bottle good Burgundy
salt
freshly ground pepper
1 small bunch parsley

Place the beans in a bowl, cover them well with cold water and allow them to stand overnight, or at least eight hours. Drain the beans, discarding the liquid, place them in a large saucepan, pour in five cups water, bring the water to a boil over a low fire, cover the saucepan, and simmer slowly for about an hour and a half, or until beans are tender but not mushy. While the beans are cooking, prepare the other ingredients. Peel the tomatoes, cut them into eighths, and remove the seeds. Scrape the carrots and dice them small. Chop the onion fine, and cut the celery leaves small. Put the bacon in a skillet, and cook it slowly until well done and crisp. Drain the bacon and crumble it. When the beans are cooked, drain them, reserving the liquid. Return beans to saucepan. Add the tomatoes, carrots, onion, celery leaves, and crumbled bacon. Measure the reserved liquid and add to it enough Burgundy to make three pints. Season with one teaspoon salt and half teaspoon pepper. Stir all well, and bring to a boil. Stir again, cover, and simmer very slowly, stirring occasionally, for one hour and a half. Cook uncovered for the last fifteen minutes. Meanwhile, remove all stems from the parsley and mince the leaves. When the soup is done, transfer it to a blender, and blend at high speed for twenty seconds. Put the contents of the blender through a kitchen strainer, discarding the residue in the strainer. Taste the soup and correct the seasoning with salt and pepper. The soup may be served at once; it may also be kept two or three days. Just before serving the soup, place it in a double boiler and heat over hot water until it is hot through. Whether served in a tureen or in individual hot soup plates, garnish with minced parsley, or pass parsley in a bowl.

SUGGESTED MENU

Well-buttered French bread is an excellent accompaniment to the soup. A mixed green salad with French dressing should follow. The wine should be the same as that used in the soup.

UN POTAGE PROVENÇAL

(*Serves 4*)

This French dish is first cousin to a fine Italian soup from Pavia. Both contain eggs poached in the soup itself. Zuppa Pavese is made with veal broth; the soup from Provence is made with a garlic broth. Traditionally, garlic soup is made with water. I am a strong believer in tradition, but in this case I think a better dish results if a light chicken stock is substituted for water. If one is going to break with tradition, one might as well break completely. This recipe does exactly that. In addition to using stock, it also thickens the soup a little. In the language of women's fashions, the changes do something for you and for the soup; unlike women's fashions it takes only about an hour to create.

16 unpeeled garlic cloves
3 pints chicken stock
14 sprigs parsley
4 whole cloves
½ teaspoon thyme
1 small bay leaf
¼ teaspoon sage
3 tablespoons olive oil
2 teaspoons salt
¼ teaspoon pepper
2 tablespoons butter
2 tablespoons sifted flour
4 eggs
4 large croutons (G)
1½ cups grated cheese

Fill a large saucepan about half full of water. Bring it to a boil, add the garlic and boil uncovered for thirty seconds. Drain, discarding water, and peel garlic. Place the chicken stock in the saucepan, add garlic, four sprigs parsley, cloves, thyme, bay leaf, sage, olive oil, salt, and pepper. Cover and bring to a boil. Reduce heat and simmer for half an hour. While soup is simmering, make a roux (G) with the butter and flour, cook, stirring frequently, for about five minutes. Add gradually to this roux about a cup and a half of the soup and stir it into a thick sauce. Bring to a boil, and add a little at a time to the soup, stirring constantly. Continue simmering. Mince the remaining parsley. When the soup is done, at the end of thirty minutes, strain it into a large, heavy skillet, discarding garlic cloves and other solid ingredients. Taste, and add salt or pepper if needed. Bring the soup to a simmer, and break and drop in the eggs, being careful to keep the yolks intact. Cover skillet, remove from fire and allow the eggs to poach for five minutes. Place a large crouton in each of four large soup plates. Remove eggs with a slotted spoon, and place one on each crouton. Pour the soup over the eggs, garnish with the minced parsley and serve with grated cheese on the side. This recipe requires only about an hour.

SUGGESTED MENU

Fresh French bread should accompany it, and Salade Flandre (G) should follow. There is a very fine rosé wine from Provence called Château Sainte-Roseline. It goes very well indeed with the soup. You could go farther and fare worse.

LOBSTER BISQUE

(Serves 2)

Candy may be dandy and liquor may be quicker, but a good meal, particularly if it has lobster in it, is more effective than either. Why lobster, the least beautiful of all creatures, should possess this singular but eminently desirable attribute is best left to biologists or psychiatrists. The fact remains, however, that what can be accomplished over, or rather after a bowl of good Lobster Bisque is astonishing. To paraphrase Conan Doyle: there was that remarkable incident after lunch at Scott's in '35; the case of the bartered bride following dinner at the Moldau in '47; the singularly easy conquest of Doctor Dottle after a meal at The Pink Cherub—of all places—in '52; and the odd arrangements in Greenwich Village hard upon a repast at Gallows' in '58. The list is much longer, of course, but the interesting point is that each of these meals included Lobster Bisque. No one could guarantee similar results after serving Lobster Bisque, but the trend would appear to be in that direction. For obvious reasons the recipe is for two.

To make Lobster Bisque from scratch requires time, patience, and skill. You can, however, enjoy its delights and benefits and avoid its complexities by using certain prepared foods. Whether you use the complex or the simple version, the happy results, as mentioned in the first paragraph, are never certain. One thing is certain: you and your guests will have an excellent meal.

The classic recipe for Lobster Bisque is complex and demanding, but worth the trouble in the end. Some time and trouble may be saved if the seafood dealer splits the live lobsters, removes the sand sacs and intestines, and cracks the claws.

I. Lobster Bisque (*Quick Version*)

(*Serves* 2)

2 cans Bon Vivant Lobster Bisque (10 oz. each)
1 can Canadian lobster (5½ oz.)
2 teaspoons butter
1½ teaspoons arrowroot flour
2 tablespoons cognac

Put Lobster Bisque in top of double boiler and heat over hot water. Remove any membranes from lobster and cut it into pieces about an inch long; add to Lobster Bisque. Put butter in a small skillet, melt, add flour, and make a roux (G), stirring with a wooden spoon until roux is cooked, about five minutes. Add two teaspoons cognac, and stir it into roux. Put remainder of cognac in a very small saucepan, bring to a boil, ignite, and pour into skillet. Stir frantically with long-handled spoon until well mixed, and pour flaming contents of skillet into Lobster Bisque. By now the soup should be hot through. Serve at once in hot soup plates.

II. Lobster Bisque (*Traditional Version*)

(*Serves* 2)

2 lobsters (1¼ lbs. each)
1 carrot
1 medium onion
8 tablespoons butter
bouquet garni (G)
  (½ teaspoon thyme
  1 bay leaf
  3 sprigs parsley)
4 tablespoons cognac
1 bottle champagne
7 cups fish stock
3 tablespoons flour
1 cup heavy cream
salt
freshly ground white pepper
red vegetable coloring

Remove coral, if any, and liver from lobster. Set aside. Cut lobsters, except claws, into sections about two inches long. Scrape the carrot and dice small. Peel and mince the onion. Put three tablespoons butter in a large saucepan. Add onion and carrot and cook over a moderate flame, stirring from time to time until onion is golden. Meanwhile, make bouquet garni. Put the lobster claws, pieces, coral, and liver into the saucepan, and cook, maneuvering the lobster pieces now and then, over a high flame for about ten minutes or until lobster shells are bright red. Heat two tablespoons cognac, ignite, and pour over lobster. When the flame dies, add one and a half cups champagne and the bouquet garni. Cover, and simmer for twenty minutes. Remove lobster and set aside to cool. Discard bouquet garni. Strain contents of saucepan and reserve broth. Add enough of the remaining champagne to broth to make one cup, and fish stock to make a total of two cups. Put three tablespoons butter in another saucepan, melt, add flour, and make a roux (G). When roux is cooked, about five minutes, add the champagne, stock, and broth mixture and cook over a low fire to make a Velouté Sauce (G). While sauce is simmering, remove meat from lobster claws, and cut into small pieces. Reserve. Take rest of lobster meat from shells and put into another bowl. Break up lobster shells, and put in a large saucepan. Add remainder of fish stock, cover, and simmer one hour and a half. Strain broth from saucepan, discarding shells. Put lobster meat, except that from claws, into broth. Put broth into blender, and blend at high speed for forty-five seconds. Strain through colander, reserving broth and discarding any residue left in colander. Heat Velouté Sauce, add broth and cream, and stir well. Just before soup starts to simmer—it must never be allowed actually to simmer—taste, and correct seasoning with salt and pepper. If color is too pale, add half a teaspoon red vegetable coloring and mix well. Put in remaining cognac, two tablespoons butter, and reserved claw meat. Heat over a low fire until butter has melted and been absorbed. Stir well and serve forthwith.

SUGGESTED MENU

Well-buttered and hot French bread should be served with the soup. It should be accompanied or followed by either a mixed green or an artichoke salad (G). Under the circumstances, the wine can be only French Champagne.

BOUILLABAISSE

(*Serves* 6)

Of all the great fish soups in the world, Bouillabaisse, as made in Marseille, is probably the most famous. There are other recognized ways to make Bouillabaisse but the Marseille version is generally accepted as the best. Basically it is made from six kinds of fish, four of which are "hard fleshed" and require more cooking than the other two, the "soft fleshed" variety. In addition, one usually adds crayfish or spiny lobster. Unfortunately, proper Bouillabaisse demands fish indigenous to the Mediterranean not available in the United States. To make this fine soup here, one must use substitutes. The French require, above all, rascasse. The other five fish are: shapon, saint-pierre, conger eel, red mullet, and sea perch. The crustacea are spiny lobster and crabs.

To make Bouillabaisse in the United States one is, perforce, required to use what one can find at the fishmonger. The list of ingredients below will show what fish were used in testing this Bouillabaisse. In addition one can use mackerel, pike, mullet, and whiting. If eel is available, it can be used instead of squid. The essential fact is that you have spiny or rock lobster, four "hard" fish, and two "soft" ones. Your fishmonger can recommend substitutes for any of the fish listed. It requires about an hour to make Bouillabaisse if you have him fillet the fish for you.

1 medium yellow onion
3 medium tomatoes
4 cloves garlic
1 sprig fennel
3 sprigs parsley
½ teaspoon thyme
1 bay leaf
1 spiny lobster tail or rock lobster tail (8 oz.)
2 squid (total 8 oz.)
½ pound perch
½ pound trout
½ pound rock fish
½ pound bluefish
1 small piece dried orange peel
1 teaspoon saffron
½ cup olive oil
1 teaspoon salt
½ teaspoon freshly ground pepper
½ pound porgy
½ pound boneless shad fillet
½ bottle dry white wine

Peel and chop the onion small and the tomatoes coarsely. Place in a large, heavy soup kettle. Add the garlic either minced or put through a press. Toss in the fennel, parsley, thyme, and bay leaf. Cut the lobster tail into pieces about an inch long and add them to the kettle. Remove and discard the heads of the squid. Skin and clean them. Chop into one-inch lengths. Place the squid alongside the lobster. Cover with three pints water and place kettle over a moderate flame. Bring to a boil. Reduce heat. Cover kettle and simmer. Meanwhile, chop the fish into half-inch lengths. This should take about five minutes. Remove kettle from the fire and add the perch, the trout, the rock, and the bluefish. Place orange peel on top of fish. Sprinkle with saffron and pour on the olive oil. Season with salt and pepper. Add additional water to cover and simmer over a moderate flame for ten minutes. Put in the porgy and the shad. Add the wine. Simmer for another eight minutes. The Bouillabaisse is now ready to serve.

A somewhat richer version of Bouillabaisse can be made by substituting fish stock (G) for water. It requires about thirty-five minutes to make fish stock but will add little to the total time for making Bouillabaisse. The fish stock may be cooking while you are preparing the other ingredients. Follow the directions given above but substitute fish stock for water.

SUGGESTED MENU

There are two ways of serving Bouillabaisse. One is to separate the fish and seafood from the broth and serve the two separately. The other, obviously, is to serve them together. I prefer the latter method. Hard, crusty French bread is really the only possible choice in that department. Any salad accompanying Bouillabaisse should be light. A mixed green salad naturally suggests itself. The wine almost certainly should be white, preferably Chante-Alouette, if you are fortunate enough to find it.

MINESTRONE MILANESE

(*Serves* 6)

What Onion Soup is to France, what Borshch is to Russia and the Catskills and what Gazpacho is to Spain, Minestrone is to Italy. The recipe for Minestrone varies from province to province as do the recipes for many other national soups. This recipe from Lombardy has been selected because it is simple, despite the length of the table of contents, and requires only about three hours to prepare and cook, once the beans have been soaked. Of all the vegetable soups—and no cookbook dealing with soup can omit that category—Minestrone is the richest. Compared to it, many other vegetable soups are poor and anemic things. It has well been said that "brandy is for heroes." Minestrone Milanese does not aspire so high, but it could claim successfully to be for the heroically hungry. It is one of the world's great peasant dishes.

The quantity yielded by this recipe is ample for six reasonably hungry people, particularly if the soup is preceded by an antipasto as suggested below. Four people might be able to eat all of it, but they would not be hungry again for a long, long time.

The only ingredients which require any time in the preparation of Minestrone are the beans and the stock. Various food companies sell a canned white kidney bean called *cannellini* which solves the bean problem and makes a very good soup. Most commercial beef broth is excellent. In this particular recipe I prefer to substitute bacon for salt pork, but either will do. While ditali is the best pasta for Minestrone, it is not the only one. Vermicelli, cut into one-inch lengths, may be used, or even elbow macaroni.

In and about Milano the chefs and housewives—who in this instance are probably as proficient as any soup cook in a Milanese restaurant—make their Minestrone as in II. Version I follows:

I. Minestrone Milanese (*Quick Version*)

(*Serves* 6)

3 slices bacon
1 large clove garlic
1 medium onion
1 leek
1 teaspoon olive oil
1 tablespoon tomato paste
3 stalks celery
1 can tomatoes (20 oz.)
1 medium turnip
bouquet garni (G)
  (1 teaspoon basil
  1 teaspoon orégano
  4 sprigs parsley)
6 cans beef broth (10 oz. each)
1 medium cabbage
2 medium zucchini
1 cup ditali
½ can baby carrots (16 oz. per can)
1 can cooked whole potatoes (4 oz.)
2 cans cooked cannellini (16 oz. per can)
4 tablespoons grated Parmesan cheese

Dice bacon. Mince garlic or use a press. Chop the onion and leek small. Put olive oil in a large soup kettle, add garlic, bacon, onion, and leek, and cook over a gentle flame, stirring from time to time, until contents are lightly browned. This should take about twenty minutes. Between stirrings, mix tomato paste with two tablespoons water; discard tops of celery and cut stalks into half-inch squares. Drain tomatoes, reserving juice, and chop tomatoes coarsely. Peel and dice turnip. Make bouquet garni. When contents of kettle are brown, add tomato paste, celery, turnip, beef stock, tomatoes, and reserved tomato juice. Put in the bouquet garni, cover, bring to a boil, and simmer very gently for about fifteen minutes. Meanwhile, discard coarse outer leaves of cabbage, remove core, and shred cabbage fairly small. Wash zucchini, but do not peel, and cut into coarse dice. Add cabbage, zucchini, and ditali to soup pot. Stir well and continue to simmer. Cut carrots into thin rounds, and potatoes into small dice. Drain the cannellini. Five minutes before serving, add the carrots, potatoes, cannellini, and cheese. Cover, simmer until hot through, and serve with additional grated cheese on the side.

II. Minestrone Milanese (*Traditional Version*)

(*Serves* 6)

½ pound dried white Italian beans
2 ounces salt pork
1 large clove garlic
½ medium head cabbage
2 zucchini
bouquet garni (G)

1 small onion
1 medium leek
1 teaspoon olive oil
1 tablespoon tomato paste
3 large Italian tomatoes
3 stalks celery
2 medium carrots
2 medium potatoes
1 small turnip
(1 teaspoon basil
1 teaspoon orégano
4 sprigs parsley)
2 quarts beef stock
½ teaspoon pepper
4 tablespoons grated Parmesan cheese
1 cup ditali

Soak beans overnight, or at least eight hours, in cold water. Drain beans and place in a large saucepan. Cover with three quarts lightly salted water. Bring to a boil, cover, and simmer one hour. Drain beans, discarding liquid, and set aside. While beans are cooking, prepare the other ingredients. Cut the salt pork into small dice, put garlic through a press, or peel and mince very fine. Mince onion and leek. Put the olive oil in a large soup kettle, heat, and add salt pork, onion, leek, and garlic. Cook slowly, stirring from time to time, until everything is lightly browned, about twenty minutes. Between stirrings, mix tomato paste with two tablespoons water, peel tomatoes, remove seeds, and chop coarsely. Discard celery tops and cut celery into half-inch lengths. Scrape the carrots and cut into dice, peel potatoes and dice them, peel turnip, and dice it. Discard thick outer leaves of cabbage and core. Shred cabbage small. Wash zucchini, but do not peel. Cut it into coarse dice. When contents of kettle are lightly browned, add tomato-paste mixture, stir, and continue to cook for five minutes. Make bouquet garni. Add tomatoes, celery, carrots, potatoes, turnip, cabbage, and zucchini to kettle. Pour in bouillon, add pepper, the bouquet garni, and grated cheese. Cover, and simmer for forty-five minutes. Add the ditali, and continue to simmer, stirring now and again, for seven minutes more. Add cooked beans, simmer another three minutes, remove bouquet garni and discard. Serve soup in hot plates.

SUGGESTED MENU

Instead of a salad to follow the soup, try a light antipasto to precede it. Obviously, antipasto presupposes that some form of pasta will follow, and normally pasta and soup are not served at the same Italian meal. It is well in most instances to follow tradition, but one need not be hidebound about it. In this case, tradition should be flouted. Serve each diner with a plate on which are tastefully arranged a few crisp leaves of lettuce and:

½ hard-cooked egg, garnished with paprika
1 slice salami
3 flat anchovy fillets
1 sardine
1 scallion
1 small stalk celery
1 ripe olive
1 large stuffed olive
2 baby artichoke hearts in oil
2 slices pimento
2 slices cucumber

Provide a cruet of olive oil, or the oil from the artichoke hearts; a cruet of white wine vinegar or three lemons cut into wedges; a salt shaker, and a pepper grinder so that each guest may flavor his antipasto to suit himself.

Warm Italian or French bread with butter should accompany both the antipasto and the soup. Plenty of grated Parmesan cheese should be available with the soup. There is a splendid, unpretentious—what a wonderful word for this purpose—Italian white wine called Cinque Terre which will add greatly to the conviviality of the occasion.

ZUPPA PARMIGIANO CON PEPPERONI
(Soup with Cheese and Sausage)
(*Serves 4*)

"When in Rome, do as the Romans do," is said to have been the advice given by St. Ambrose to St. Augustine. This very practical bit of philosophy pertained to matters theological and was intended to assist St. Augustine in avoiding difficulties that might arise from failure to follow the customs of the city. However useful the dictum may have been theologically, it does not apply to culinary matters. Recipes can be changed without putting St. Ambrose's admonition to the proof. Stracciatella alla Romana is a very famous and wonderful Roman soup. It is served frequently in Rome and elsewhere in Italy as an opening course for meals. It lacks, however, the body to constitute a meal by itself. One who is extremely fond of Italian cooking believes that this soup could be "porked up" to make a good main dish by adding sausage.

This soup is a borderline case. It can be prepared in about an hour. Attempts to shorten this time are hardly worth the effort.

6 ounces pepperoni
2 quarts chicken stock
½ cup Soave (Italian white wine)
6 eggs
¾ teaspoon orégano
1 cup grated Parmesan cheese
4 sprigs watercress

Slice pepperoni very thin and quarter each slice. Put chicken stock in a large saucepan and bring to a boil. Place pepperoni in hot chicken stock, add wine, cover, and simmer for fifteen minutes. While pepperoni is simmering, break eggs into a bowl. Beat eggs vigorously. Add orégano and cheese gradually and beat until cheese is dissolved. When pepperoni has cooked its allotted span, approximately fifteen minutes, bring chicken stock to a boil and continuously but hesitantly add contents of mixing bowl, beating the soup frantically with a wire whisk until soup is hot through; take care not to let it boil. Unless egg-cheese mixture is made an integral part of the soup, it will separate. It will still be good, but will not look it. Taste and correct seasoning. If soup is too thick, thin to desired consistency with additional hot chicken stock. Garnish each serving with a small sprig of watercress and serve very hot.

SUGGESTED MENU

Because of the soup's consistency, the best bread to go with it would be Italian bread sticks. One excellent salad could be made from finocchio, tomatoes, and chicory with a French dressing (G) to which is added a clove of garlic. The wine, of course, will be the same used in making the soup.

SAUERKRAUT SOUP

(Serves 4)

"Revolting," my wife said when I suggested Sauerkraut Soup. She dislikes sauerkraut intensely: I like it, particularly with turkey or frankfurters; but I confess the idea of making soup from it gave me a two-minute pause. I thought to myself that it is as Austrian and peasant as onion soup is French and peasant. For generations all classes of Austrians, including the Hapsburgs, have sought after and dined happily on peasant soups. "If," I thought, "if it was good enough for the Emperor of Austria, it is good enough for me." Having come to this conclusion after the pause, I hied myself to the kitchen and prepared the soup. To her surprise and mine, my wife enjoyed it. So did I. So will you.

Austria is one of the great ski centers of middle Europe. With the possible exception of a hot buttered rum, nothing could be more welcome after an exhilarating morning on the slopes than a generous plate of steaming sauerkraut soup. A short nap and back to the ski lift. J. P. Marquand had one of his characters say: "A man can be dangerous indeed with twenty volumes of Voltaire behind him." The quotation is reminiscent of a remark made by

Peterkin Pepit, who said, "With a plate of Sauerkraut Soup inside him a man could scale Mont Blanc and ski down the other side in an afternoon."

Made with raw ingredients this soup takes not quite two hours to prepare. The time can be reduced by more than 50 percent by using already cooked potatoes and sauerkraut, as in I. The traditional version is, in this instance, the better and, if time allows, should be used. It will be found under II.

I. Sauerkraut Soup (*Quick Version*)

(*Serves 4*)

3 slices bacon
1 large onion
3 teaspoons tomato paste
½ teaspoon paprika
¾ teaspoon caraway seed
6 cups strong beef stock
1 can boiled small potatoes (16 oz.)
2 generous cups canned sauerkraut
12 cocktail frankfurters
salt

Dice bacon and place in a skillet. Cook over a low flame. While bacon is cooking, dice the onion, and add to the skillet. Cook slowly until onion is golden and soft. Meanwhile place tomato paste in a small bowl and mix well with three quarters cup water. When the onion is cooked, add to the skillet the tomato-paste mixture, paprika, caraway seed, and two cups of stock. Mix everything well and simmer, covered, for ten minutes. While skillet simmers, drain potatoes and chop into small dice. Drain the sauerkraut. Place it and the diced potatoes in a large saucepan or soup kettle. Add the remaining beef stock and the contents of the skillet. Cover and heat over a low flame. Now cut the frankfurters in half, lengthwise. Toss them into the pot and continue heating until very hot through. Taste, add salt if needed, and serve forthwith.

II. Sauerkraut Soup (*Traditional Version*)

(*Serves 4*)

2 generous cups raw sauerkraut
6 cups strong beef stock
3 slices bacon
1 large onion
3 teaspoons tomato paste
½ teaspoon paprika
¾ teaspoon caraway seed
1 large potato
12 cocktail frankfurters
salt

Place the sauerkraut in a heavy pot. Add two cups stock, cover, and simmer for half an hour. Meanwhile dice the bacon and the onion. Put the bacon in a skillet over low heat. As soon as a thin film of fat has appeared, add the diced onion and continue to cook until the onion is golden, stirring from time to time. While the bacon and onion are cooking, put three-quarters cup water in a small bowl, add the tomato paste, and stir until it dissolves. When the onion is cooked, add the tomato paste, paprika, caraway seed, and two cups stock. Stir well and continue to cook for about ten minutes. Add the contents of the skillet to the pot. Mix well, cover, and simmer slowly for about twenty minutes. Meanwhile peel the potato, dice it, and soak the dice in cold water for five minutes. Drain the potato, add it to the soup pot, cover, and bring to a slow boil. Boil for half an hour longer. Slice the frankfurters lengthwise. At the end of the half hour, add the frankfurters and remaining stock. Continue cooking long enough to heat the fresh stock and the sausage. Taste, add salt if required. The soup is ready to serve.

SUGGESTED MENU

The obvious salad is Hofburg (G) and the bread should be Austrian too: Viennese rolls would make a real contribution to the meal. A pleasant and appropriate white wine would be Grinzinger. Serve it slightly chilled but not cold.

BRAMBORÓVA POLÉVKA KYSELÁ
(Potato Soup with Sour Cream)

(*Serves 4*)

It is truly remarkable in what mysterious ways soup recipes travel to perform wonderful things at your table. Mention is made elsewhere (Section VIII) of the peregrinations of Jade Soup Mary Dulaney Hunter. The recipe for Bohemian soup has traveled even further although it has undergone fewer additions, substitutions, and other sea changes. It started out in the capital of the ancient kingdom of Bohemia and traveled overland and by ship to Sydney. There it rested for a while and then, following the route of Phineas Fogg, who went around the world in eighty days, it crossed the broad Pacific. It arrived, as all good things do, in San Francisco. Later it moved reluctantly away from that great city, for a brief time, to Chicago. It then found its way to Alexandria in Virginia. From there its owner very kindly gave it to me, and I take great pleasure in sharing it with you.

1½ pounds potatoes
1½ teaspoons salt
1½ teaspoons caraway seed
3 eggs
6 slices bacon
3 small leeks
1½ teaspoons butter
1½ pints sour cream
1½ tablespoons flour
3 tablespoons chopped parsley
salt
pepper

Peel and dice potatoes. Place them with salt and caraway seed in a heavy saucepan and add three cups water. Bring to a boil. Cover, and simmer until potatoes are soft, about thirty minutes. Meanwhile, hard-cook the eggs and sauté the bacon until done, but still soft. Chop the leeks. Place butter in another small skillet and cook leeks until soft. Mix the sour cream and flour together in a bowl. As soon as the eggs are cool enough to handle, peel them and dice. When the potatoes are done, remove the saucepan from the fire. Add the sour cream and flour mixture and the leeks. Stir well. Bring to the boiling point. Remove from the fire again and run through a blender at high speed for fifteen seconds. Return to saucepan. Add the hard-cooked eggs and bacon. Heat thoroughly over a low flame. Taste, correct seasoning, and serve in hot plates garnished with chopped parsley.

SUGGESTED MENU

The donor of this recipe explains that rye bread is the normal accompaniment in Bohemia, or anywhere else. For salad, I understand the Czechs would use plain lettuce with thinly sliced cucumbers sprinkled with fresh parsley, served with a dressing of vinegar, water, and small quantities of salt, sugar, and pepper. This salad, of course, should be served with the meal. According to my informant, Czechs seldom drink wine with this kind of meal. He suggests beer.

TRANSYLVANIA PEASANT STEW

(*Serves 4*)

I had thought of naming this dish after Transylvania's most famous nobleman, Count Dracula. However, I thought my readers might be chary of trying a soup named after a vampire. Under these circumstances it seemed better to call it exactly what it is: a soup prepared by the peasants of that forbidding area, once a part of Hungary, then of Rumania, and, by the time this book is published, it could well be part of some other country. Irregardless, as the pundits do not say, of the area's rulers, the peasants will still be there, as they have always been, and the soup will still be a staple of their diet, and a very good staple too. There is not too much difference between this recipe and that for a more widely known Hungarian dish: *gulyas*. I once had a most unfortunate experience with that dish. A well-meaning friend who had lived in Budapest gave me a recipe for it. In those dear dead days, I did not know that, unless otherwise specified, anything simmered had to be covered. While waiting for the goulash to cook, my friend and I drank sazeracs. Result: the stew was never finished and we could not have eaten it had it been. But that has nothing to do with this recipe. I have not attempted *gulyas* since. The soup is excellent.

Despite its excellence, Transylvania Peasant Stew is time consuming because you start with raw meat. If this dish were cooked in the kitchen of Count Dracula, it could be made in much less time. It is generally believed that he liked his meat very rare. If your tastes do not run in that direction, you can make a rapid version of the stew which has the additional merit of economy. This soup is an excellent way of using leftovers in a nutritious and appetizing dish. In this case, the required leftover is roast beef, preferably medium rare, although that is not too important. If you happen to have some roast or boiled potatoes remaining from a previous meal, they may be utilized too. If cooked beef is not resting happily in the refrigerator, you can procure it from the neighborhood delicatessen. Have it cut in slices half an inch thick.

Those who never have leftover roast beef or who detest delicatessens—a curious detestation—or prefer traditional peasant dishes as the peasants make them, will enjoy trying their hands at the traditional version, II.

I. Transylvania Peasant Soup (*Quick Version*)

(*Serves 4*)

- 1 medium onion
- 1 large red pepper
- ½ pound calf's liver
- 2 tablespoons butter
- 1 tablespoon bacon fat
- 4 tablespoons paprika
- 3 tablespoons sifted flour
- 1 cup good red wine
- 1 can whole white potatoes (16 oz.)
- 3 ½ inch slices cooked roast beef
- 2 cans concentrated beef broth (10 oz.)

Chop onion and red pepper small but do not mince. Cut calf's liver into cubes approximately a quarter inch on a side. Place butter and bacon fat in a large, heavy saucepan, add chopped onion and pepper, and cook over a moderate fire until soft. Stir to prevent browning. Add calf's liver. Brown quickly on all sides. Mix one tablespoon paprika and the flour in a small bowl, and add to the saucepan. Stir it in well, and make a roux (G), cooking for about four minutes. Add wine, mix well, cover, and simmer very gently for twenty minutes. Meanwhile, drain potatoes, reserve liquid, and cut potatoes into half-inch cubes. Chop the roast beef the same size. At the end of twenty minutes, add the potatoes, the potato liquid, roast beef, and one and a half cans beef broth. Stir well, continue to heat. When it is warm, remove half a cup of liquid from the saucepan and mix it with the remaining paprika. Return this paste to the saucepan, mix it well and, when the soup is hot through, it will be ready to serve. If it is too thick—it should be fairly thick—thin with some reserved beef broth. Add no salt.

II. Transylvania Peasant Soup (*Traditional Version*)

(*Serves 4*)

- 1 onion
- 2 pounds lean beef
- 1 tablespoon butter
- 1 tablespoon bacon drippings
- 4 tablespoons paprika
- ½ pound sliced calf's liver
- 3 tablespoons sifted flour
- 2 teaspoons salt
- 1 cup good red wine
- 1 large red pepper
- 1 pound small potatoes

Mince onion, not too fine. Remove fat and gristle and cut lean beef into three-quarter-inch chunks. Put butter and bacon fat in a large, heavy saucepan or soup kettle. Melt butter, and add minced onion. Cook gently, turning occasionally, until lightly browned. Stir in one tablespoon paprika. Add beef, and stir well until meat is browned on all sides. Halfway through this process, put in the liver. When all is browned, sprinkle with flour, stir well, add one teaspoon salt and the wine, and stir again. Cover, and simmer one hour. While soup is simmering, seed the red pepper and chop into half-inch pieces. Peel the potatoes and cut into half-inch cubes. At the end of the hour, remove saucepan from fire, take out liver, and mince it. Return it to the saucepan, add the chopped pepper, cover the pan, return to fire, and simmer another hour or an hour and a half, until the beef is tender. Meanwhile, place the cubed potatoes in another saucepan, sprinkle with one teaspoon salt, cover with water, and cook slowly until potatoes are almost done. Drain potatoes, reserving the water in which they were cooked.

Keep the potatoes warm. When beef is tender, add potatoes, remainder of the paprika, and enough of the reserved potato water to make a fairly thick soup. Heat through and serve in hot plates or a hot tureen.

SUGGESTED MENU

A Hofburg Salad (G) would make this an extremely wholesome and filling meal. As it was designed to be eaten in the shadow or on the slopes of the Carpathians, it is a perfect combination for a cold day. Unless you want to go to the trouble of making spaetzle, the approved farinaceous accompaniment is hard Vienna rolls. About the wine there can be little question; Egri Bikavér is obvious. If that is unavailable, substitute any reasonably good claret.

SOUPA LAKHANIKA
(Vegetable Soup)
(*Serves* 6)

As you will remember, Byron wrote of "the Isles of Greece, the Isles of Greece! Where burning Sappho loved and sung." Loving and singing are all very well in their place but to do these things satisfactorily one must also be well fed. This would account for the fact that Greece has contributed much to cookery.

Because of a bad press, Greek cooking, outside of Greece, has a poor reputation. In a small Maryland town there was once a restaurant operated by one whose name could well have been Achilles Aristides. Across his window was emblazoned: NO GREEK COOKING. It was probably a wise precaution at that time and place. To judge Hellenic food, however, by what is served in many American restaurants is unjust to proper Greek cookery and may well deprive the judge of some fine meals. Many of the small tavernas in Athens, for example, serve excellent meals for very few drachmae.

Sometime after Marco Polo returned from his tour of the Celestial Kingdom, Venetians traded with and occupied parts of Greece. They took with them recipes for pasta, which explains why vermicelli came to be included in this recipe for a Hellenic vegetable soup.

Here again is another example of a dish whose quick version compares favorably with the traditional one. The difference in taste and consistency would be noted only by those with the most sophisticated of palates. The quick version follows. For those who prefer "the Greek way," version II will be their cup of tea, to mix a metaphor.

I. Soupa Lakhanika (*Quick Version*)

(*Serves 6*)

1 medium onion
½ cup olive oil
1 small cabbage, about ¾ lb.
1 can cooked tomatoes (20 oz.)
2 quarts chicken stock
1 teaspoon salt
1 teaspoon freshly ground black pepper
2 ounces vermicelli

Peel and mince onion. Put olive oil in a heavy saucepan or soup kettle. Heat over a low flame. When oil is hot, add onion, and cook slowly until onion is golden but not burnt. Stir occasionally. While onion cooks, shred cabbage small, discarding hard core—sounds Communist but is not—drain tomatoes, reserving juice, and chop tomatoes coarsely. When onion is done, add cabbage, tomatoes, tomato juice, chicken stock, salt, and pepper. Cover and bring to a boil. Reduce heat, and simmer, covered, not too gently, for twenty minutes. Break vermicelli into one- or one-and-a-half-inch lengths. At the end of twenty minutes, taste, and correct seasoning. Add vermicelli, stir well, and continue to simmer another ten minutes. The soup is now ready to serve in hot plates.

II. Soupa Lakhanika (*Traditional Version*)

(*Serves 6*)

1 medium onion
¼ cup olive oil
2 medium tomatoes (about ¾ pound)
1 small head cabbage (about ¾ pound)
7 cups chicken stock
1 teaspoon salt
½ teaspoon freshly ground pepper
2 ounces vermicelli

Peel and mince onion. Put olive oil in a large saucepan. When oil is hot, add onion and cook slowly, stirring occasionally, until onion is golden. Meanwhile skin and chop the tomatoes coarsely, and shred the cabbage. When onion is cooked add the chicken stock and tomatoes. Season with salt and pepper. Cover, and bring to a boil. Reduce heat and simmer for one hour and a half. Break the vermicelli into quarters and add it and cabbage to the soup. Stir well. Continue to simmer for another fifteen minutes. The soup is ready to serve in hot plates.

SUGGESTED MENU

Because the soup contains pasta, no bread is required. Make a simple salad by cutting a large head of lettuce into quarters; garnish each with three or four Greek olives, a small square of Feta cheese, and a few strips of pimento. Serve with French dressing (G). The wine, of course, will be well-chilled Retsina.

BORSHCH

(*Serves 8*)

Nothing Russian, be it a negotiation or the making of Borshch, should be entered into lightly. Some doubt exists about the origin of Borshch. There are many different recipes, in which beets and cabbage are the only common ingredients, and almost as many different spellings of the name. One can be sure only that this soup is definitely a peasant dish. Internal evidence clearly indicates that Borshch is one of those soups which were made in a pot kept on the back of the stove, and into which were tossed, from time to time, leftover meat and vegetables. Such soups are almost invariably of peasant origin and are almost invariably excellent for both the body and the soul. That Borshch is of Russian origin is generally accepted among most gastronomes. Hence the rather unusual spelling of the name. I am assured by Peterkin Pepit's dear Russian friend, Madame Leeotard Perkinsky, that it is an accurate transliteration from the Cyrillic.

Borshch is an ideal one-dish meal for cool or cold weather. By discarding the beef after cooking, eliminating the duck and the sausage in II (traditional version) and then chilling the soup, you will have a good cold dish. Not so rich or delicate as Vichyssoise, perhaps, but a fine meal. Whether it is hot or cold, sour cream should always be served with it.

Despite the recommendation that cooks should allow a minimum of six hours for Ukrainian Borshch, it is possible to make a fine shorter version. It may not have the Slavic impact of the longer version but few moujiks would prefer one version to the other. Each is authentically Ukrainian. Madame Perkinsky, an expert with the knout, persuaded her chef to part with this old recipe (II). The persuasion was not too arduous as he admitted to having thirty-two methods of making Borshch. The two recipes suggested here are extremely interesting. Although seemingly different, the difference is more apparent than real. Why not try each of them? Attempt the quick version when you are in a hurry, and the traditional version when you have eight hours which you would like to spend in the kitchen. A good idea is to make either version the day before you plan to serve the soup. Borshcht, like most peasant soups, improves with age—within reason. For a quick but excellent Borshch, try the following:

I. Borshch (*Quick Version*)

(*Serves* 8)

1 pound lean pork
1 large onion
2 tablespoons butter
½ can tiny whole carrots (16 oz. per can)
2 cans midget whole beets (16 oz. each)
1 can tomato juice (16 oz.)
2 ounces vodka
1¼ cups sour cream

Cut pork into half-inch cubes, and cut onion small. Melt butter in a skillet and add chopped onion and pork. Cook until onion is soft and pork is well browned on all sides. Toss frequently. While pork and onions are cooking, drain carrots, and mince. (Remainder of carrots and juice may be placed in refrigerator for another occasion.) Drain beets, reserving juice. Mince beets. When pork and onion are done, place contents of skillet in a large saucepan. Add reserved beet juice—it should be about one cup—two and a half cups water, and tomato juice. Cover, and simmer slowly for twenty minutes. Add chopped carrots, and beets. Simmer for five minutes. Put in vodka, and continue to simmer until soup is very hot. Garnish each serving with two tablespoons sour cream and present to your guests, exclaiming "Slava Bogu! 'tis done!"

II. Borshch (*Traditional Version*)

(*Serves* 8)

3 leeks, green only
2 medium carrots
1 pound beets
1 medium onion
½ pound white cabbage leaves
2 celery stalks
12 tablespoons butter
bouquet garni (G)
(6 sprigs parsley
2 teaspoons marjoram
2 teaspoons dill seed
18 peppercorns)
2 pounds brisket of beef
5 pints chicken stock
1 pound chipolatas, or Polish sausage
½ roasted duck
salt
pepper
1½ pints sour cream

Wash the leeks well. Scrape the carrots. Peel beets, and onion. Slice onion thin, and cut slices in half. Cut the leeks, carrots, half the beets, cabbage, and celery into julienne strips. Cut the remainder of the beets into fine dice. Place diced beets in a saucepan with one quart water, bring to a boil and simmer about one hour. Meanwhile place the butter in a large saucepan or soup kettle, and cook the julienne vegetables slowly for about half an hour or until soft. Make bouquet garni. Cut the beef into one-inch cubes. When the vegetables in the saucepan are soft, pour in three pints of stock, add the bouquet garni and the beef. Bring to a boil, cover, and simmer about one hour. The beet dice should now be done. Strain the liquid through cheesecloth and reserve. Mash the beets through a strainer as much as possible and strain the juice through cheesecloth, adding it to the liquid in which beets were cooked. You should have about one pint. Discard the beet residue. Grill the chipolatas until well browned on all sides. While they are cooking, cut the duck meat into pieces about a half inch square; discard bones and skin. Chop the chipolatas into half-inch rounds. When the soup has cooked four hours, remove from fire. Take out the cubes of beef. When they are cool, remove and discard the bouquet garni and all fat from meat. As soon as the soup has cooled enough, skim fat from the liquid. Return saucepan to fire. Add the remaining stock, the beef cubes, duck, chipolatas, and beet juice. Heat gently until hot through. Taste, and correct the seasoning with salt and pepper. The soup should be served very hot, with sour cream on the side.

SUGGESTED MENU

The perfect accompaniment to Borshch is black bread. The salad should be kept simple. A plain mixed green salad, with a few tomatoes added and a simple French dressing (G), complements the soup extremely well. Wine presents a bit of a problem. Because one hesitates to drink vodka throughout a meal—at least I do—and Russia apparently exports no wine fit to drink, it would seem that wine might be omitted. Why not start the meal with a couple of gulps of chilled vodka, or with a vodka martini, and forget about wine with the soup? I doubt that Russian peasants ever had wine with their Borshch.

RASSOLNIK

(*Serves 4*)

Most people who have not spent any time in Russia and many who have think Borshch is the only soup eaten in that country. This belief, of course, is not correct as there are a great many different soups which originated in the various parts of what is now the Soviet Union. The interesting fact, however, is that "borshch" actually means "soup" in old Russian but through the decades has come to mean a particular kind of soup as described in the immediately preceding recipe. One of the other Russian peasant soups which has much merit is Rassolnik. Unlike Borshch, it can be cooked in about sixty minutes, and it also makes a hearty meal. Its origin is lost amid the many provinces of Russia, and in the few remaining kitchens of the moujiks. It is, therefore, unnecessary to raise the red flag or the clenched fist or to sing the "Internationale" before sitting down to eat it.

As a matter of fact, one of the untold tales of Baron Münchhausen deals with a remarkable exploit about 1765; at an inn in Smolensk, he won a wager of one thousand gold rubles by eating a tun (252 wine gallons) of Rassolnik for supper. It is believed that his memory never recovered.

3 small cucumbers
4 large potatoes
1 large onion
6 lamb kidneys
2 tablespoons butter
1 tablespoon sifted flour
3 pints chicken stock
6 large sprigs parsley
salt
pepper

Peel cucumbers. Cut one into large pieces and extract and reserve juice by putting through a fruit or vegetable press. Slice the other cucumbers vertically. Discard seed portion, cut the rest of the cucumber into half-inch dice. Peel the potatoes and cut into one-fourth-inch dice. Peel onion and mince. Remove all fat and gristle from kidneys and slice very thin. Melt butter in a small skillet. Add onion and cook until soft. Put in kidneys and brown over a low flame. Add flour and make a roux (G), cooking about four minutes, stirring from time to time. While roux is cooking, warm chicken stock in a saucepan. When roux is done, gradually add one cup of stock to the skillet. Cover, and simmer ten minutes. Add cucumber juice, the diced cucumbers, and potatoes to the remaining chicken stock. Gradually pour in contents of skillet. Simmer until potatoes are done, about twenty minutes. While soup is simmering, mince the parsley. When potatoes have cooked, add parsley, taste, and correct seasoning with salt and pepper. The soup should be served very hot.

SUGGESTED MENU

Russian or any other type of black bread, including pumpernickel, is excellent with the soup although, because of the potatoes, it is not essential. A salad of leeks, cooked beets, and lettuce with Russian dressing (G) would be both appreciated and good. In Tsarist days, of course, Russian nobility is alleged to have drunk nothing but French champagne. It is hard to believe that this was the only wine. The peasants drank vodka. You make your own selection.

IV

EASTWARD

NUPTIAL SOUP

(*Serves 4*)

This soup is a perfect example of the difficulty of tracing the origin of any soup, or indeed any dish, which is found in the Near East. The fact that it contains lamb is good evidence that it is a soup from that area. It could, however, be Greek or Turkish, Rumanian, Bulgar, or even Russian. Regardless of its origin, it is usually considered a "nuptial soup" and is frequently served after weddings, probably because it contains cumin. Aside from its use as a condiment, cumin is believed by some to have the virtue of preventing husbands from straying. Why it should be thought necessary to include it in a wedding soup is beyond my comprehension. My observations would indicate that it would be better to serve the soup on the third or fourth wedding anniversary. Another herb, turmeric, adds a certain amount of flavor and provides an appealing color. Avoid getting it on your hands. In addition to being an excellent herb it is an equally good dye.

The traditional version of this soup (II) is, in my opinion, superior to the quick version (I). The shorter method makes a fine meal and needs no apology. It also has the additional virtue of using up that half leg of lamb which has been sitting in your refrigerator since last Saturday night. If you have to start with fresh lamb and have the time, the results of the traditional version will be even better.

If possible, lamb stock should be used, but the combination of beef broth, chicken stock, and water makes a good substitute.

I. Nuptial Soup (*Quick Version*)

(*Serves 4*)

3 pounds roast lamb
1 can condensed beef broth (10 oz.)
3 cups chicken stock
1 medium onion
1 large carrot
6 tablespoons butter
5 tablespoons flour
2 teaspoons ground turmeric
2 teaspoons ground cumin
⅛ teaspoon cayenne pepper
2 lemons
4 egg yolks
salt
pepper

Discard all fat, bone, and gristle from the lamb and cut it into half-inch cubes. Place the broth in a large saucepan. Add six ounces stock. Put in the lamb. Cover, heat over a very low flame. Peel and mince the onion. Scrape the carrot and cut into fine dice. Melt butter in a skillet and cook onion and carrot until soft. Meanwhile, mix flour, turmeric, cumin, and cayenne. Sprinkle the mixture over the contents of the skillet. Mix it well and cook slowly for four minutes to make a roux (G). Add to the skillet two cups of stock and cook slowly, stirring, to make a sauce. Gradually add sauce to the heating soup. Peel the lemons, reserving the peel, and squeeze the juice into a small bowl. Beat the egg yolks and stir them into the lemon juice. Gradually add this mixture to the soup, stirring energetically all the time. Cut the lemon peel into very small pieces, not more than a fourth of an inch square. Add these to the soup. Taste, and correct seasoning with salt and pepper. Heat through, and serve.

II. Nuptial Soup (*Traditional Version*)

(*Serves 4*)

4 pounds neck of lamb
1 medium onion
1 large carrot
6 tablespoons butter
6 tablespoons flour
1 teaspoon ground turmeric
1 teaspoon ground cumin
⅛ teaspoon cayenne pepper
2 lemons
4 egg yolks
salt
pepper

Remove as much fat as possible from the lamb, discard, and cut lamb into one-and-a-half-inch pieces. Place in a large kettle. Add two and a half quarts water and cook over a low heat. Peel and mince the onion. Scrape and cut the carrot into dice. Place onion and carrot in the kettle with the lamb and continue to simmer for two and a half hours until the lamb is very well done. Remove lamb from pot, reserving the broth. Allow lamb to cool. While the lamb is cooling, melt the butter in a skillet. Mix the flour with the turmeric, cumin, and cayenne. Add to the butter and make a roux (G). Remove as much grease as possible from the contents of the saucepan, and remove and discard all bones, fat, and gristle. Cut meat into half-inch cubes. Peel the lemons, reserving rind, and squeeze lemon juice into a bowl. Beat the egg yolks and stir into the lemon juice. When roux is cooked, gradually add about 1½ cups broth from the pot and cook to make a thick sauce. Return the lamb cubes to the kettle. Gradually stir in the sauce. When soup is hot through, add the egg and lemon mixture, stirring violently over a low flame to prevent scrambling the eggs. Mince the lemon peel very fine and add to the soup. Stir, taste, and correct seasoning with salt and pepper.

SUGGESTED MENU

Probably the best salad with this soup is mixed greens with very thin tomato slices and thinly sliced cucumber, with a French dressing. For bread, rolls well covered with sesame seed are ideal for taste and in the best tradition. In the matter of drink, if you assume that the soup is Turkish in origin, you will serve coffee, as most Moslems do not consume alcohol. Otherwise, any reasonably good rosé will go very well.

MULLIGATAWNY

(*Serves 4*)

Translated literally, mulligatawny—an Indian word—means "pepper water." It is not to be confused with firewater, which derives from a different kind of Indian. The people who invented this soup speak Tamil and are found throughout the southern part of India and in Ceylon. They are proud of their language, justifiably so, and given to riot and insurrection when efforts are made to subordinate it to another tongue. The Tamils are and should be proud of their soup, knowledge of which was brought to the West by Englishmen returning from the subcontinent. As with most dishes indigenous to an area but which have spread widely, many variations occur in the recipe. This version is English.

Properly made, Mulligatawny lives up to its name, but its inherent heat can be controlled by adjusting the quantity of curry powder and cayenne pepper. The two following recipes provide a fairly mild dish. In making the traditional version (II), the meat should be mutton. If that is not available, lamb should be substituted. The meat should not, however, be baby spring lamb. In devising the quick version of the soup (I), I have tried to provide one solution for a perennial kitchen problem: the use of leftovers, particularly meat. Hash, of course, is always with us, but it has unfortunately —hash can be a succulent dish—become a kind of joke. To put leftovers on the table in appetizing form and to conceal the fact that they are what they are, few things could be better than Mulligatawny Soup. Almost any kind of meat—lamb, veal, or beef—can be used. In an emergency even chicken or turkey might be substituted, although this is not recommended.

I. Mulligatawny (*Quick Version*)

(*Serves 4*)

- 2½ pounds cooked lamb
- 2 medium onions
- 2 tart medium apples
- 1 medium turnip
- 1 can cooked baby carrots (10 oz.)
- 1 tablespoon bacon fat
- 3 tablespoons butter
- 1 tablespoon curry powder
- 4 tablespoons sifted flour
- ½ teaspoon cayenne pepper
- 3 cans beef broth (10 oz. each)
- 1 quart chicken stock

Remove and discard all fat and gristle from meat, and cut it into half-inch cubes. Reserve. Peel onions, apples, and turnip, drain carrots, and chop all into medium dice. Place bacon fat and butter in a large saucepan. Melt butter, add diced onions and turnip, and cook over a slow fire for about ten minutes, turning occasionally. While vegetables cook, mix curry powder, flour, and cayenne pepper well in a small bowl. Add apples and carrots to saucepan, and cook another five minutes. Put in the flour-curry-pepper mixture, and make a roux (G), cooking a further five minutes, and stirring often to prevent scorching. Meanwhile, mix the beef broth and chicken stock and bring to a boil. Remove from heat. When roux is cooked, add the mixture, a little at a time, stirring constantly to prevent lumping, and make a smooth, slightly thick soup. Put in the meat cubes, stir well, bring to a boil. Allow to boil gently, still stirring, for about two minutes. Reduce heat, cover, and simmer soup for thirty minutes. It is now ready to be served, or it can be refrigerated and kept for two or three days.

II. Mulligatawny (*Traditional Version*)

(*Serves 4*)

2 medium onions
2 tart apples
2 carrots
1 turnip
2 pounds lean stewing lamb
bouquet garni (G)
  (3 sprigs parsley
  1 bay leaf
  1 teaspoon dried thyme)
2 tablespoons flour
1 tablespoon curry powder
½ teaspoon cayenne pepper
1 teaspoon salt
1 teaspoon lemon juice

Peel the onions and apples. Peel the carrots and turnip. Chop all four into coarse dice. Set aside. Remove all fat from lamb, and cut the lean meat into three-quarter-inch cubes. Put the fat into a large, heavy saucepan and render it slowly until there is enough liquid fat to cover the bottom of the saucepan generously. Remove and discard remaining fat. Put in the chopped vegetables and apples, and cook over a very slow fire for about ten minutes. Turn frequently to coat all ingredients and to prevent burning. While contents of saucepan are cooking, make bouquet garni. Add to the saucepan flour, curry powder, and cayenne pepper, mix well, and cook for five minutes, stirring constantly. Add meat, salt, the bouquet garni, and two quarts water. Place over high heat and bring to a boil. When the liquid boils, skim to remove the scum which will rise. Reduce heat, cover, and simmer for three hours. Check about once an hour to remove any scum. At the end of three hours, add lemon juice, stir in, and serve soup in hot plates.

SUGGESTED MENU

The obvious bread to serve with it also comes from India and is called "pappadums." These are very thin, highly seasoned, crisp, circular wafers varying from six to ten inches in diameter. They are not unlike tamales and can be bought cooked or semi-cooked. They are served in India with curries. In addition to these uses, pappadums make unusual and very good cocktail snacks. Salade Flandre (G) has just the right amount of crispness and acidity to contrast with the soup. Wine, if any is served at all, should be red, light, and dry.

DAHL

(*Serves 4*)

Dahl is a Hindu soup. For that reason, of course, it contains no meat as the only Hindus who eat meat are the Sikhs. Hence, it is an extremely useful dish for lunch or supper for guests who are observing Lent or for others who may be vegetarians by conviction rather than by faith. One of the great advantages of this soup is that even for carnivorous animals such as I it makes an excellent dish and it can be served with complete assurance to any company.

With skill and attention, Dahl may be cooked in an hour. With very little skill, the soup can be prepared readily in seventy-five minutes. One version would seem to meet the requirements of this book. The finished product should be on the thick side, about the consistency of a full-bodied Dutch pea soup. If thinning is required, use water. The recipe calls for quick-cooking split peas.

1 cup yellow split peas
1 teaspoon salt
2 tablespoons turmeric
2 medium onions
1 medium green pepper
4 tablespoons butter
3 tablespoons curry powder
1 tablespoon allspice
1 clove garlic
1 teaspoon lemon juice
Bombay duck (G)

Wash the peas until the water is clear. Place them in a large saucepan. Add four cups water, the salt, and the turmeric. Bring to a boil. Cover, and simmer for fifty minutes. Chop onions and green pepper coarsely. Melt butter in a skillet. Add the onions, green pepper, curry powder, and allspice. Mince the garlic fine or put it through a press and add to the skillet. Cook over a moderate heat, stirring frequently, until the onion is slightly brown. Add lemon juice and cook five minutes longer. Add contents of the skillet to the saucepan. Stir well, taste. Then add salt as required. The operation of chopping and cooking the contents of the skillet should not require much more than twenty minutes so that time is left for preparing the Bombay duck. This should be chopped into one-half-inch squares and approximately two tablespoons should be placed in each of four saucers. When the soup is served, fairly hot, a saucer of Bombay duck should be available to each diner so that he may sprinkle his soup as he wishes.

SUGGESTED MENU

Pappadums or brown bread should be served with the soup along with a salad consisting of very thinly sliced cucumbers and cherry tomatoes, attractively arranged on a few lettuce leaves. Make a dressing consisting of one part Spice Islands Beau Monde seasoning, and three parts lemon juice. Allow each guest to dress his own salad. Besides being vegetarians, Hindus also have a "down" on alcoholic beverages. To be traditional, therefore, Darjeeling tea should be served with the meal. If you prefer wine, a rosé would probably be the best choice.

ONION SOUP ARBELA

(*Serves 4*)

When one thinks of onion soup, one's mind naturally turns to France, not to Persia. While France has no monopoly on any soup, French chefs have made Soup à l'Oignon one of the famous dishes of the world. The Persians, however, made onion soup probably before Julius Caesar was dividing Gaul into three parts. While there is no indication of the age of this Iranian recipe, it is obviously derived from the peasantry and probably is of great antiquity. It makes a superb meal.

You can but wonder what the outcome at Arbela would have been had Darius fed his host such a repast before he joined action with Alexander. Probably the outcome would have been an even greater victory for the Macedonians. I can think of nothing which is so relaxing and so soporific as this great Persian dish. It can be prepared in approximately sixty minutes. No short version is necessary.

6 medium onions
6½ tablespoons butter
4 tablespoons sifted flour
¾ teaspoons turmeric
2 teaspoons salt
1½ teaspoons black pepper
4 large sprigs fresh mint
¾ cup lime juice
¾ cup lemon juice
⅓ teaspoon cinnamon
2 eggs

Peel and slice the onions thin. Place butter in a large saucepan or soup kettle and melt over a low flame. Add the onions and cook over a moderate fire, stirring frequently, for six minutes. Add flour and continue to cook, stirring from time to time, for about four minutes to make a roux (G). Pour in six cups of water, add turmeric, one and one-half teaspoons salt, and one teaspoon pepper. Stir well, cover, and simmer for thirty-five minutes. Meanwhile, chop the mint very fine. Prepare the lime juice and the lemon juice. At the end of thirty-five minutes, add lime and lemon juice, mint, and cinnamon. Simmer another ten minutes. Beat the eggs well. Just before serving, remove the saucepan from fire and add the eggs, stirring the soup madly. Taste, and correct seasoning with remaining salt and pepper.

SUGGESTED MENU

In lieu of bread, a small quantity of cooked rice could be added to the soup. In my opinion, however, this tends to make the soup too thick and adds little to its taste. In the absence of real Persian bread, hard club rolls would be quite acceptable. The proper drink, of course, would be mead. Unfortunately, mead is almost unobtainable in the United States—unless you keep bees and make your own. The nearest equivalent to mead is probably Traminer, either imported or domestic. It should be served chilled.

A MESS OF POTTAGE

(*Serves* 6)

This is the most famous soup in Christendom. We know little about it except that it was made of red lentils and by a con man who did his red-haired brother out of his inheritance. So I thought, at least, until I had eaten lentil soup. Now I am less positive that Esau got the worst of the bargain. I have no idea of his birthright's ingredients, but I know the ingredients of lentil soup. When one is hungry, it is superb; when one is not hungry, it is still good. You cannot make lentil soup without a ham bone. If you wonder how Jacob happened to have one, remember that the Mosaic code was not promulgated until after the Exodus. Regardless of dogma, once you have made and eaten a mess of pottage, you will find that Esau fared quite well.

An ingredient almost always lacking in commercial lentil soup, and which can turn a good soup into a delicious one, is smoked, hot sausage. For this purpose, the best variety I have found is made in Baltimore (properly and locally pronounced "Balmer") by Messrs. Schluderberg and Kurdle. The sausages are sold as "Little Hot Shots." Baltimore is famous for a number of reasons including Francis Scott Key and his well-known anthem; a traditional gourmet approach to food; and monuments. Modesty forbids mention of another reason. "Little Hot Shots" should be added to this list.

The total time required to make this soup in the traditional manner is three to three and a half hours. A somewhat similar soup, lacking some of the body and flavor of the original, can be put together—I use the term advisedly—in about twenty minutes. It is important that you use the soups listed below, or very similar ones. The first is a thin soup with many lentils and vegetables; the second is almost a purée with fewer whole lentils. They complement each other perfectly.

If you use the longer method, you must, by tradition, employ red lentils. Whether you soak them overnight or for only an hour will depend on the instructions on the box. Once the lentils have been soaked, proceed as in II.

I. A Mess of Pottage (*Quick Version*)

(*Serves* 6)

- 3 cans Progresso Lentil Soup (20 oz. each)
- 3 cans Bon Vivant Lentil Soup (13 oz. each)
- 2 packages Little Hot Shots (4 oz. each)

Place the soups in a large saucepan; chop the sausages into half-inch pieces; add to the saucepan. Bring to a boil, and allow to simmer slowly, stirring from time to time, until the soup is hot through. Serve at once.

II. A Mess of Pottage (*Traditional Version*)

(*Serves* 6)

- 1 box Smith's lentils (1 pound)
- 3 slices lean bacon
- 3 medium carrots
- 1 largish onion
- 2 large stalks celery with leaves
- 1 large clove garlic
- 1 ham bone with some ham on it
- 2 bay leaves
- 6 cloves
- ¼ teaspoon cayenne pepper
- 1 teaspoon black pepper
- 4 tablespoons minced parsley
- 2 packages Little Hot Shots

Prepare lentils according to box instructions. Place the lentils in a large soup kettle. Add three quarts water. Dice bacon, and place it in a medium skillet. While the bacon is cooking over a low flame, dice carrots, onion, celery with the leaves, and place all the vegetables in the skillet with the bacon. Put the garlic through a press and mix it well with the vegetables. Cook the vegetables slowly for ten or twelve minutes, until the onion is soft. Meanwhile, remove as much meat as you can from the ham bone, discarding all fat and gristle and chopping the remainder coarsely until you have one cup. Cut or break the bone into pieces to fit your kettle. Add the bone, the contents of the skillet, bay leaves, cloves, cayenne, black pepper, and parsley. Cover, and place the kettle over a high flame. While it is coming to a boil, chop the sausages into half-inch slices. Throw them into the kettle. When it comes to a boil, skim if necessary, reduce heat, and allow the soup to simmer slowly for about an hour and a half, stirring occasionally. At the end of that time, check the soup for consistency. Skim if necessary. If soup is too thin—it should be quite thick when done—continue to simmer with the lid off for another thirty minutes. Check again. If the soup is still too thin, continue simmering until it is thick enough for your taste. If it is too thick, add water. Remove and discard ham bone and bay leaves. Serve the soup very hot in hot soup plates.

SUGGESTED MENU

No matter which method you use, this mess of pottage is quite substantial, and you will require only a simple salad with French dressing. A mixed green salad seems to fit this bill. Bread of any kind is, I think, unnecessary. As for wine, I suppose one should serve Manischewitz in keeping with the pottage's tradition, but that is a little on the sweet side. Why not settle for a couple of bottles of Charles Krug's cabernet?

SCHAV (SORREL) SOUP

(*Serves 4*)

By skipping over a number of centuries but staying in the same place geographically, we can make a more modern Israeli soup which has great merit. It is not so good as A Mess of Pottage nor is it quite so filling. It is, therefore, more appropriately served in the spring and early fall than is lentil soup. It has the additional merit of being simple to prepare and quick to cook. Because most of the ingredients, with the exception of sorrel or spinach, can be found in the average pantry, it is an excellent dish to serve when you have to prepare a lunch or supper at short notice.

Schav is sorrel. When this is not available, it may be replaced quite satisfactorily with spinach. The difference in taste is small, but sorrel should be used when possible.

One of the great advantages of Schav Soup is that it may be served either hot or cold. A second advantage lies in the fact that this soup, although filling, is a very simple and rapid dish to prepare. If hot, it should be served immediately when done. If cold, make it at least three hours before serving and refrigerate it.

1 pound fresh sorrel or spinach
2 medium potatoes
4 scallions
2 quarts chicken stock
2 tablespoons dill
½ tablespoon tarragon
2 tablespoons lemon juice
1 teaspoon salt
¼ teaspoon freshly ground pepper
8 eggs

Wash greens thoroughly and remove all grit. Remove stems and chop leaves coarsely. Peel potatoes and cut into small dice. Slice the scallions small. Place the chicken stock in a large saucepan. Add sorrel or spinach, potatoes, scallions, dill, and tarragon. Bring to a boil. Reduce heat. Cover, and simmer about twenty minutes. Add lemon juice, salt, and pepper, and simmer ten minutes longer. Meanwhile, put eggs in a bowl along with three cups water and beat until very light. Slowly and quietly ladle half of the soup stock into the egg mixture, beating continuously with a wire whisk to prevent the eggs from cooking. Remove soup from the fire and add egg mixture to it. The soup is now ready to be served.

SUGGESTED MENU

Matzoh or unleavened bread is the obvious accompaniment for the soup. A compatible salad is made from cucumbers and onions. Peel and thinly slice two large cucumbers and cut onion into thin rings. Place together in a bowl. Cover them with a dressing made of one-half vinegar and one-half water, a teaspoon of salt, and a tablespoon of sugar. Stir, chill, and stir again before serving. It is heresy, but with this soup I like well-chilled Retsina. Any other light, white, and dry wine will serve equally well.

OYSTER SOUP ASTARTE

(*Serves 4*)

Many years ago when gasoline rationing compelled multiple fares in taxis, a friend of mine and I managed to flag down a hack in which a brawny foremast hand was already ensconced. He had the most beautiful black eye I have ever seen. Joseph's coat and Solomon's glory were poor and shoddy things in comparison. My friend and I had been discussing potables before we hailed the cab and, once in, continued. We wound up the subject to our satisfaction. To be sociable, I said to the sailor, "And what does the Navy drink?" He growled simply, "Southern Comfort." I asked why, and he replied, "I dunno, but it makes the girls give in easy." I never had to test his theory but suspect it has the same validity as another fond belief about the similar virtues of oysters and Champagne. That theory has been tested in various ways and combinations and, to be Biblical again, "found wanting." This particular combination of soup ingredients, however, had not been put to the proof when the sailor mentioned "Southern Comfort." Because it might have some virtue, and to help it along in that direction, it has been named after a well-known Carthaginian goddess.

If the fish stock is already made, the soup can be prepared in less than an hour, and in about an hour and a half if you have to make the fish stock. You may substitute for the stock two and a half pints clam juice mixed with a pint of dry white wine.

- ¼ pound butter
- ⅔ cup sifted flour
- 3 pints fish stock
- 1 cup heavy cream
- 2 egg yolks
- 1 teaspoon fresh lemon juice
- ¼ teaspoon cayenne
- 1 teaspoon salt
- ½ teaspoon freshly ground white pepper
- 2 quarts medium oysters
- ½ bottle Champagne
- paprika

Melt butter in a large, heavy saucepan. Add flour to make a roux (G). Cook, stirring, until roux turns golden, but does not brown. While roux is cooking, warm fish stock. When roux is done, gradually add fish stock, stirring constantly, until soup is smooth. Cover, and simmer very gently for twenty minutes, stirring every five minutes. While soup is a-simmer, place cream in a small bowl, add egg yolks, and beat well. When soup is done, remove from fire and skim off the scum. Add four tablespoons of soup to the egg-cream mixture. Stir well. Add mixture to the soup, along with the lemon juice, cayenne, salt, and pepper. Return to a moderate flame, and, stirring constantly, cook about four minutes, but do not allow soup even to simmer, let alone boil. Remove soup from fire but keep warm. It should be moderately thick.

Drain oysters well, but do not wash. Just before serving soup, place drained oysters in a skillet. Cover with champagne, and poach them slowly, turning frequently, until they are almost done, i.e., when they are plump and the edges are just beginning to curl. Strain oysters, reserving the poaching liquid. Add oysters to soup, return soup to a low flame, and gradually add enough liquid from the skillet to bring the soup to the consistency of heavy cream. As soon as soup is hot, transfer to hot soup plates or a hot tureen, sprinkle generously with paprika, and serve at once.

SUGGESTED MENU

You should serve hard rolls with it, and champagne. In lieu of rolls hard oyster crackers known as "Trentons" may be substituted. All of this is fairly substantial fare, of course, hence the salad should be light. Salade Flandre (G) would be a good choice.

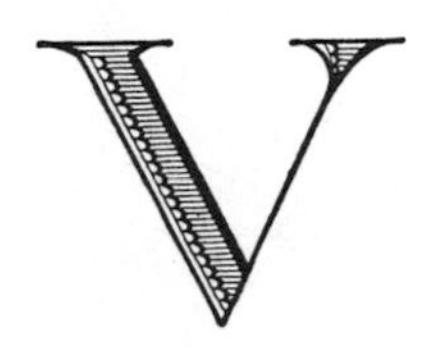

FARTHER EAST

POTAGE MONGOLE
(*Serves 4*)

Peterkin Pepit after one of his trips across the Gobi—he traveled widely—claims to have found a recipe for Potage Mongole in a yak-skin tent in the middle of the desert. The internal evidence would indicate that the tent must have been occupied by a well-traveled European, as few inhabitants of Mongolia, Inner or Outer, are likely to have been familiar with pea soup, cream of tomato soup, or sherry. Despite questioning by his many friends, Pepit insisted that that was the origin of the recipe. A certain famous American explorer, who made many trips in the area, may have left it behind in an abandoned camp, although he was not particularly noted for leaving anything behind. The recipe that was brought back from the desert was written in Mandarin, a language with which Pepit, naturally, was thoroughly familiar. It is to him, therefore, that we are indebted for this celestial recipe.

Dr. Dottle pointed out to his friend Pepit that this soup would take an inordinately long time to make and he doubted very much that the renowned American explorer had ever really made it. Pepit pointed out to his friend Dottle, in turn, that perhaps the renowned explorer, who obviously carried most of his food in cans, had made his Potage Mongole by combining canned soups. Pepit tried it and pronounced it excellent. Pepit's rapid version is found below under I. It is followed under II by a variation of what Pepit translated from the Mandarin.

I. Potage Mongole (*Quick Version*)

(*Serves 4*)

2 cans Cream of Tomato Soup (10 oz. each)
2 cans Cream of Pea Soup (10 oz. each)
2½ cups milk

Dilute each can with ½ can milk. Mix soups in a saucepan and heat over low flame, stirring from time to time. If the soup is still too thick, thin with a little more milk.

II. Potage Mongole (*Traditional Version*)

(*Serves 4*)

2 small leeks
2 tablespoons butter
3 cups Habitant Pea Soup (p. 11)
3 cups cream of Tomato Soup (p. 35)
1½ cups milk
½ cup dry sherry
¼ teaspoon cayenne pepper
salt
black pepper
4 teaspoons minced parsley
small croutons (G)

Wash the leeks well, chop small. Melt butter in a small skillet. Add leeks. Cook over a moderate flame, stirring occasionally, until the leeks are soft, about five minutes. Meanwhile, place both the soups in the top of the double boiler and heat over water and moderate flame, stirring constantly with a wire whisk to remove all lumps. When leeks are soft, remove from fire and add a half cup milk. Mix well and place mixture in blender and blend at high speed for thirty seconds. Strain through kitchen strainer and add resulting liquid to the double boiler. Add remaining milk, sherry, and cayenne. Stir well, taste, and correct seasoning with salt and pepper. Heat soup over hot water until hot through. Serve in hot soup plates. Garnish each plate with minced parsley. A bowl of croutons should be placed beside each diner.

SUGGESTED MENU

With the croutons, of course, you will need no bread. If you believe in the origin of the soup, serve Celestial Salad (G) with or after it. Wine can be either warm sake or a cool rosé.

KHAO THOM PLA
(Fish and Rice Soup)
(Serves 4)

A physical anthropologist, obviously a friend of mine, who spent two years in Siam (now known as Thailand) working for the Siamese government was kind enough to give me the recipe for this soup. More, he cooked it for me so that I would know how it should taste when properly prepared. There is an area in Bangkok known as "Raja Wongs" which made a specialty of serving this soup to people after the theatre or the cinema. I gather that people returning from those places, or other forms of entertainment, would stop and order the soup brought to them in their cars, a kind of Oriental drive-in or diner. The sight of Siamese girls as car hops added, I am told, considerably to the occasion. This will be understood by anyone who has ever had an opportunity to see young Siamese girls.

Whether served by car hops or in a restaurant, Khao Thom Pla should always come in four bowls. The first and largest bowl contains the soup itself. The three others contain, respectively: fried garlic, Chinese parsley, and croutons. If Chinese parsley is not available, it may be omitted. The garlic is essential and the croutons are, if such a word exists, semi-essential. Do not be put off by the quantity of garlic. When sauteed, it loses much of its objectionable odor. Unlike many Oriental soups, this dish may be prepared in less than an hour. Have your fishmonger fillet the fish and give you the heads and bones, from which you may make the fish stock as described in Section I.

1 cup raw rice
24 cloves garlic
¼ pound Chinese parsley
¼ cup Wesson oil
7 cups fish stock
2 small perch
3 small black bass
4 tablespoons fish shoyu sauce (G)
small croutons (G)

Place a quart of water in a saucepan. Bring to a boil and add rice. Cover, and continue to boil slowly until rice is done, approximately thirty minutes. While rice is cooking, peel garlic and cut into small dice about one-quarter inch on the side. Scrape the parsley and chop into half-inch cubes. Place oil in a skillet. Heat over a low fire. When hot, toss in the garlic cubes and cook until crisp. Remove from skillet and drain on paper towels. When rice is done, drain, and wash. Put the fish stock in another saucepan. Bring to a boil and add rice. Continue to cook, covered, until rice is almost mush. Meanwhile, back at the chopping board, cut the fish into three-quarter-inch squares. Just before the rice is mushy, about twenty minutes, add the fish and the shoyu sauce. Continue to boil gently for another five minutes and serve very hot in soup plates. Put at each place three small bowls—one containing the fried garlic, another the chopped parsley, and the third the croutons, so that each diner may sprinkle the soup as he desires.

SUGGESTED MENU

An excellent way to start this meal is by serving sliced black eggs, which may be procured at the same Chinese store at which you bought the parsley and the fish shoyu sauce. Garnish each egg slice with a small piece of ginger root. Obviously no bread should be served with the soup, but it could well be followed or accompanied by a dish of tiny, sliced, cold cucumbers and chopped watercress neatly attired in French dressing (G). Tea is the obvious choice but a vin rosé would be equally good as a beverage.

VEGETABLE SOUP CANTONESE

(*Serves 4*)

Among the questions which have bothered philosophers and theologians over the centuries are: the difference between right and wrong, how many angels can dance on the point of a needle, and which came first, the chicken or the egg? This is a comparatively short list. Another question can be added. Did the Chinese invent minestrone—under another name, of course—or is it strictly an Italian creation? It is well known, as is mentioned elsewhere in this book, that pasta was brought from Cathay to Italy by Marco Polo. Pasta is integral to minestrone. The following Chinese vegetable soup, using Chinese vegetables, also has a basic ingredient pasta noodles. These, however, are made from beans and are, therefore, not, properly speaking, pasta, a derivative of wheat. So we find our philosophers and theologians faced with still another problem. Whether the problem is solved or not, the soup which raised it is excellent. Like the preceding recipe, it can be made well within an hour, so that only one version is provided.

1 medium tomato
1 small Chinese cabbage
⅓ large green pepper
1 large stalk celery
1 jar cooked chicken (5½ oz.)
1 cup snow peas
6 scallions
4 ounces bean thread noodles
1 can sliced bamboo shoots (5½ oz.)
2 quarts chicken stock
1 teaspoon monosodium glutamate
½ teaspoon black pepper
1 tablespoon soy sauce
1 cup bean sprouts

Peel and chop tomato coarsely. Shred enough Chinese cabbage and chop pepper small to make one-half cup each. Cut celery and chicken into small dice. Chop snow peas in half, and cut scallions into half-inch lengths. Using scissors, cut the noodles into one-inch lengths. Drain bamboo shoots, discard liquid. Place the chicken stock in a large saucepan or soup kettle. Add the green pepper and the noodles and simmer for five minutes. Add monosodium glutamate, pepper, and soy sauce. Put in remaining ingredients. Cover, and simmer over a low flame fifteen minutes longer. Taste, and add more soy sauce or pepper as needed.

SUGGESTED MENU

In view of the fact that, properly speaking, there is no starch in this soup, it is suggested that the dish could be preceded by egg rolls and mustard and followed by a simple salad of sliced cooked beets and shredded lettuce with French dressing (G). Strong tea, in this instance, both with and after the soup, would be better than wine as an accompanying drink.

BOK TOY TONG MIT PORK BALLS AVEC CREVETTES CON POLLO

(*Serves 4*)

This is a kind of international soup, in name only, to be sure. I do not know the Chinese for pork balls, shrimp, or chicken. The recipe is said to derive from a Cantonese cookbook of considerable antiquity. Travel to and from south China being what it is makes original research on the subject hazardous if not impossible. Internal evidence from the soup itself and from the consumer shows that it is in the tradition of Cantonese cookery. What more could be demanded of any dish?

Although soup is served in China at the end of the meal, some say to fill up the abdominal interstices left by other food, this particular soup makes an admirable main course for an informal lunch or supper. It gains face because it may also be used as a well-flavored clear broth before the main course at dinner. Reduce the number of pork balls and chicken chunks to one each and the shrimp pieces to three per cup; strain out and discard the Chinese cabbage and the scallions. The result is an excellent and unusual vegetable bouillon for a formal meal.

Bok Toy Tong *et al.* can be made, everything included, in about an hour. No attempt to save time would be feasible or worth the effort.

6 cups chicken stock
2 chicken breasts, boned
1 small Chinese cabbage
12 slender scallions
½ teaspoon monosodium glutamate
1 tablespoon ground ginger, or finely minced ginger root
2 teaspoons soy sauce
½ teaspoon salt
½ pound ground lean pork
1 tablespoon cornstarch
1 tablespoon rice wine (sake)
24 peeled green shrimp

Place the chicken stock in a large saucepan, add chicken breasts, and simmer twenty minutes. Remove and reserve chicken. While chicken is cooking, shred enough of the cabbage small to make three cups, and set aside. Chop the scallions into half-inch rounds. Add to the chicken stock: the cabbage, the scallions, monosodium glutamate, ginger, soy sauce, and salt. Bring to a boil and simmer, covered, for twenty minutes. While the soup is simmering, put the pork into a bowl, add the cornstarch and rice wine. Mix well with the hands and form into balls about three-quarters of an inch in diameter. Reserve. Chop shrimp into thirds, and cut chicken into chunks. At the "small" end of twenty minutes, put chicken chunks and pork balls in the soup, re-cover saucepan, and continue to simmer twelve minutes more. Then add the shrimp, and simmer another five minutes. The soup is ready to serve.

SUGGESTED MENU

While New Orleans and Canton are far apart, Pontalba Salad (G) makes a good accompaniment to the soup, which is comparatively thin and can take a rich salad. Bread raises a bit of a problem. The Chinese, except to the north, use rice rather than bread. (One hesitates to recommend "rice crispies.") Any good crusty bread will solve this problem. Wine is no problem: more of that used in the soup, and served pleasantly warm.

SHARK'S FIN SOUP

(*Serves 4*)

One of the most famous Chinese dishes—indeed, one of the most famous soups in the world—is Shark's Fin Soup. Its taste is unique. Except for the time involved, it is comparatively easy to concoct. There are two ways to make it: the short version, which requires between two and a half and three hours; the traditional one, which requires about twenty hours and should be divided between two days. The methods are identical, except that the short version employs already cooked and canned shark's fins; the other starts with raw fins. To my shame, I have never used the raw fins, partly because they are difficult to obtain and partly because I am lazy. If starting with the raw materials makes a better soup, then, indeed, the Celestial Kingdom deserves that name for this soup alone if for no other reason. The quick version is heavenly enough.

It is extremely dangerous and rather foolish to say this is the greatest soup in the world. One cannot compare the wines of Burgundy with those of Bordeaux, or those of the Rhône with those of the Rhine. One is tempted, of course, to say after eating a superlative meal, "This is the best food I ever ate." At the moment the statement may be true. But it is perilous. I am trying not to say that Shark's Fin Soup is the finest soup in the world. But the length of this note is sufficient indication of the strength of the temptation.

The recipe presented here is the quicker one, based on already cooked shark's fins.

1 large chicken breast, split
2 cans boiled shark's fins (15 oz. each)
4 scallions
8 tablespoons sake
4 teaspoons ground ginger, or finely minced ginger root
1 slice boiled ham, ¼ inch thick
1 teaspoon salt
1 teaspoon freshly ground pepper
3 teaspoons monosodium glutamate
1 large can sliced bamboo shoots, drained (10 oz.)
2 tablespoons soy sauce
3 pints rich chicken stock
1 cup cooked rice

Place chicken in large saucepan. Barely cover with water and simmer for twenty-five minutes. Drain the shark's fins, place them in a skillet, and barely cover with water. While water heats, chop the scallions into half-inch lengths and add to skillet along with four tablespoons sake and two teaspoons ginger. Cover and boil gently for fifteen minutes. Drain the shark's fins and rinse thoroughly. When chicken is done, remove from fire and shred the meat, discarding bones and skin. Shred the ham. Place the ham, chicken, and shark's fins in the top half of a large double boiler or steamer. Add the remaining sake and ginger. Put in salt, pepper, monosodium glutamate, bamboo shoots, and soy sauce. Cover the pan, place over hot water and cook for two hours. Combine the liquid in which the chicken was cooked with the chicken stock. Start heating the stock very slowly, about half an hour before the mixture in the double boiler is ready. Ten minutes before it is ready to serve, add the chicken stock and continue to cook until hot through. Place a quantity of rice in each of the four soup plates. Pour soup over it and serve.

If you feel that you *must* use the traditional method and raw shark's fins are available, the fins will require the following preparation. Before you start to make the soup, trim off hard pieces. Rinse fins carefully in warm water and then soak in warm water for four hours. Remove from water, rinse again, return to a saucepan, and cover with fresh water. Simmer covered for five hours. Drain and rinse in cold running water to remove all sand. Cut out and discard all bones. Place fins in a steamer, cover, and steam over water for five hours more. Drain and rinse again. This time, remove and discard all skin. The shark's fins should now faintly resemble thin Chinese bean noodles, and are now ready to be used in lieu of the two cans of boiled shark's fins listed in the foregoing recipe. It is, I think, better to be content with already prepared and boiled shark's fins.

SUGGESTED MENU

No bread is required. It will not be missed. Salads are eaten very little in China but this dish is improved if it is followed by one. Try Celestial Salad (G). The drink obviously will be warm sake.

BIRDS' NEST SOUP

(*Serves 4*)

Birds' or Swallows' Nest Soup is probably more famous, because more easily available, than Shark's Fin Soup. Sometimes the most interesting story connected with food is that of the how, the when, and the why a particular dish was first eaten. One wonders who was the first brave and very hungry man who ate a lobster. One could go on for pages wondering about the courage, the imagination, and the amount of hunger necessary to make someone experiment with oysters, squid, snails, rattlesnake, or some varieties of large insects much esteemed in certain parts of the world. No such problem exists in the case of Birds' Nest Soup, at least according to legend.

It became part of Chinese cuisine when Genghis Khan overran most of China in the thirteenth century and forced the Chinese emperor with a small group of retainers to take refuge on a little island which produced almost no food. In order to keep alive, the emperor and his court were compelled to eat soup made from swallows' nests, which were plentiful. This particular kind of swallow's nest is available in the United States; it can be bought in Chinese grocery stores, cleaned and packaged. Because of this, it is possible to prepare this magnificent dish in about two and a half hours. Confronted with fresh swallows' nests, the cook would find himself in much the same position as he would be if confronted with fresh shark's fins.

4 ounces birds' nests
1 slice boiled ham ¼ inch thick
parsley (to make 2 tablespoons minced)
3 teaspoons cornstarch
3 egg whites
2 tablespoons sake
3 pints rich chicken stock
3 tablespoons soy sauce
2 teaspoons monosodium glutamate

Place birds' nests in a bowl, cover with water, and soak one hour. While nests are soaking, dice ham and mince parsley. Place cornstarch in a small bowl. Add a half cup water and stir into a paste. When nests are soft, drain in a colander and wash in running cold water. Add birds' nests to the saucepan. Cover with water and boil gently for one hour. Meanwhile, place the egg whites in a bowl. Add sake and beat until mixture begins to froth. Put chicken stock in a large saucepan. Add the soy sauce and monosodium glutamate and heat over a very low flame. When birds' nests have cooked their allotted span, drain and wash them again. Place them in the chicken stock. Gradually add, with great agitation, the cornstarch mixture. Now with the soup still bubbling, slowly stir in the egg whites and sake. Allow to simmer slowly over a very low flame until hot through. Garnish with boiled ham and parsley and serve very hot.

SUGGESTED MENU

This is one of the Chinese soups which is not helped by the addition of rice. For that reason, bread should accompany it. Almost any kind of hard roll will serve this purpose. So, as a matter of fact, will a kind of cracker known variously as "Thin Captains," "Pilot Biscuits," or "Sea Toast." Almost any salad would be a good accompaniment for Birds' Nest Soup. The beverage can either be warm sake, hot tea, or cold beer.

BEAN CURD AND MUSHROOM SOUP

(*Serves 4*)

One of the simpler but more satisfying of Chinese soups is made with bean curd and mushrooms. I was introduced to this soup years ago by Pepit upon his return from a visit to Hong Kong. He said it had been served in a small Chinese restaurant by a beautiful slant-eyed waitress. This toothsome dish—I refer to the soup—is a great boon both to the lovers of Chinese food and to those who cook it. One does not have to slave over a hot stove or addle his brains to find short cuts. Admittedly, it is not so good as the two preceding Chinese dishes but it will make a more than satisfactory meal when time presses and guests are hungry.

Dried Chinese mushrooms and bean curd can be purchased at any Chinese grocery store or market. While there is a distinct difference between Chinese mushrooms and the cultivated American variety, the latter in the form of canned mushroom stems and pieces may be substituted if the Chinese variety is not available. There is no substitute for bean curd.

2 ounces dried Chinese mushrooms
2 raw chicken livers
½ pound lean pork
1 Chinese cabbage
4 bean curds
1 can peeled water chestnuts (5½ oz.)
10 small scallions
2 quarts chicken broth
2 eggs
1 can bamboo shoots, sliced (5½ oz.)
2 teaspoons monosodium glutamate
salt
pepper
soy sauce

Put the mushrooms in cold water to soak approximately twenty minutes. While mushrooms are soaking, wash livers, remove any fat, and slice livers thin. Remove all fat and gristle from pork and chop into approximately three-quarter-inch cubes. Slice enough cabbage to make two cups. After mushrooms have soaked, drain them and wash in three waters or for five minutes in running water. Cut bean curds into half-inch cubes. Slice water chestnuts coarsely. Cut scallions into half-inch pieces, including part of the green tops, to make half a cup. Bring chicken broth to a boil, and while it is heating beat the eggs well. Add all other ingredients to the chicken broth except the eggs. Bring to a boil again and stir in the beaten eggs gradually. Taste, and add salt, pepper and soy sauce as needed. Boil slowly ten minutes more. Serve in hot soup plates.

SUGGESTED MENU

Instead of bread with the soup, egg rolls and Chinese mustard should precede it. Celestial Salad (G) will go very well with it. Those interested in drink with their meals—who is not?—are given the choice of warm sake, hot tea, or cold beer; of the three, in this instance, I should have tea.

MOCK DRAGON SOUP

(*Serves* 6)

Snaring a dragon for soup or for any other purpose is, today, a formidable task. A man named George slew the last authentic dragon in the West, although a cognate species continued to flourish until a considerably later era in the Eastern Hemisphere. Oriental dragons then disappeared, as did the dinosaurs a hundred million years earlier, for no known reason. Some say they starved to death because they incinerated all their food before they could eat it. This hypothesis has never been proved, nor is it universally accepted. But even were dragons or their delectable flesh—the tenderest cuts were from the flame-making and flame-throwing organs—available, proper dragon soup would still be almost impossible to make. The only extant copy of the recipe for what must have been a wholesome and heart-warming dish is believed to be written in Manchu code and held in the secret archives of Kublai Khan. These are stored, some Orientalists think, in an inaccessible cave on the grounds of the Khan's pleasure dome near the mouth of the Alph, the sacred river.

While no "live" comparisons have been possible, for obvious reasons, real dragon soup, as far as is known, was similar in taste, consistency, and appearance to Mock Dragon Soup. The latter contains duck, beef, and lobster, which are symbolic respectively of the dragon's ability to fly, to walk on land, and to swim under water. The ginger and pepper combine to represent the fiery breath. If the heat is insufficient, add a bit of cayenne. Ancient biologists, who knew about such things, agree that the incinerating qualities of a dragon's breath were created by a combination of two powders secreted in separate sacs. When mixed with saliva from a third sac, they were emitted as an explosive liquid which ignited spontaneously as it left the creature's mouth. A curious error has arisen about dragons. They did not breathe flames; they exhaled them. Dragons were oviparous, and the egg drops simulate dragon eggs, much sought after in those days by children. The eggs were painted in curious designs with kohl, ochre, henna, betel-nut juice, and similar coloring material. They were exchanged with other youngsters at a movable feast which fell in what would now be called late March or early April. Mock Dragon Soup is, therefore, now most appropriately served at Easter. It is good at any time of year. Naturally the soup is served annually at the orphic meetings of the Black Dragon Society. Now one no longer has to be a member of that arcane organization to eat this celestial dish.

Someone—whose name to my shame I do not remember—once remarked that time is money. No better proof could be adduced than this recipe. If this quick version of Mock Dragon Soup is not the most expensive dish described herein, the quick recipe for Canuck Duck Soup Rivière Renard has to be. True, you can use some leftovers in its preparation, but whoever heard of leftover duck? Unless time is very important, I suggest you use the traditional version described under II and make it the day before serving. Where time permits, the traditional version makes, I believe, a somewhat more interesting soup. On the basis of cost alone, it is to be highly recommended.

I. Mock Dragon Soup (*Quick Version*)

(*Serves* 6)

2 medium carrots
2 large stalks celery
2 large leeks
3 tender leaves Chinese cabbage
2 cans wild duck consommé (10 oz. each)
½ cup orange juice
½ cup soy sauce
2 teaspoons monosodium glutamate
2 tablespoons ground ginger, or finely minced ginger root
1 teaspoon black pepper
2 rock lobster tails (8 oz. each)
½ pound lean roast beef, one half inch thick
1 can Reese's whole mallard duck, or any other canned duck
2 cans sliced bamboo shoots (5 oz. each)
3 eggs

Scrape carrots and cut into quarter-inch dice. Wash celery, leeks, and Chinese cabbage. Cut each into half-inch pieces. Place one pint water in a large saucepan, add duck consommé, orange juice, soy sauce, monosodium glutamate, ginger, black pepper, and cut-up vegetables. Put in lobster tails; bring to a boil, cover, and simmer twenty minutes. While saucepan simmers, cut roast beef into half-inch cubes. Drain duck, reserving liquid, and cut meat into chunks of approximately the same size. Drain bamboo shoots, discard liquid. Remove lobster tails, put in colander, and cool with running cold water until cool enough to handle. Remove lobster meat from shells, and discard the latter. Cut lobster into half-inch cubes. Place duck meat, roast beef cubes, lobster meat, bamboo shoots, and reserved duck juice in saucepan with the liquid. Bring all to a boil. Reduce heat to a simmer, and break the eggs one at a time into the soup. Stir well with a fork or wire whisk until eggs have become cooked drops à la Chinese egg-drop soup. Serve forthwith.

II. Mock Dragon Soup (*Traditional Version*)

(*Serves* 6)

- 2 medium carrots
- 2 large stalks celery
- 2 large leeks
- 3 tender leaves Chinese cabbage
- ½ cup orange juice
- 1 duck, cut up
- 2 rock lobster tails (8 oz. each)
- ½ cup soy sauce
- 2 teaspoons monosodium glutamate
- 2 tablespoons ground ginger, or finely minced ginger root
- 1 teaspoon black pepper
- ½-pound slice roast beef ¼ inch thick
- 2 cans bamboo shoots (5 oz. each)
- 3 eggs

Scrape carrots and cut into one-quarter-inch cubes. Wash celery, leeks, Chinese cabbage, and cut each into half-inch pieces. Place chopped vegetables in a large saucepan or soup kettle. Add orange juice, duck pieces, lobster tails, soy sauce, monosodium glutamate, and ginger. Pour in five pints water, cover, bring to a boil and simmer for twenty minutes. Remove lobster, wash in cold water, remove meat, discard shells, and reserve meat. Skim soup if required. Continue to simmer until duck is done, about forty minutes more. Cut lobster meat into half-inch cubes and set aside. When duck is done, remove pieces from soup. You will now have just under three quarts of liquid. Reduce it, by boiling, to two quarts. Place in bowl and refrigerator. As soon as duck is cool enough to handle, remove meat from bones, discarding bones, fat, and skin. Cut duck meat into pieces to match the lobster and add to the latter.

When soup has cooled—preferably overnight—skim off fat. What you do with the duck fat is your problem. It has no further interest for this soup. Return skimmed broth to saucepan, and over a moderate heat bring to a boil. Add chopped lobster and duck. While waiting for soup to boil, cut roast beef into half-inch squares, and put into soup. Add bamboo shoots. As soon as soup starts to boil, break eggs seriatim, and drop into simmering soup, one at a time. Stir soup on each occasion, with a fork or wire whisk, until eggs have become cooked drops all the same as Chinese egg-drop soup. The soup is now ready to be served, and should be, immediately, in hot plates.

SUGGESTED MENU

Instead of bread, the Chinese of the north use what the Italians call pasta; the Chinese of the south eat rice. To add either noodles or rice to this soup would be, to quote an old friend, "too much of a muchness." Instead of bread, start the meal with one egg roll per person. Although frozen egg rolls are marketed, they are inferior to the uncooked variety which can be purchased from almost any good Chinese restaurant. These should be fried, just before the meal, in deep, very hot fat, until the dough is crisp. Drain on paper towels and serve immediately with fiery Chinese mustard. This can be homemade by dissolving dry mustard in cold water in the ratio of one teaspoon of mustard to two teaspoons cold water. The mustard should be prepared at least fifteen minutes before it is needed. Hazel's Herbage (G) is a good complement to the egg roll and soup. The obvious beverage is tea, served in small handleless porcelain cups. If an alcoholic drink is a desideratum, have cocktails before or with the egg roll. Warm sake with the soup would also be good.

BOE BOE AYAM
(Malay Chicken Soup)
(Serves 4)

In the Malay States, according to Noel Coward, the natives wear hats like plates, which the local English inhabitants refuse to don. Again, according to the same authority, even the smallest rabbit in that area deplores the fact that Englishmen and certain other distinctly different types of creatures venture out at noon, a rather foolish habit. One cannot speak, of course, for the other creatures, but one rather suspects that the Englishmen are on their way to lunch on this succulent chicken soup. I have never been in the Malay States, nor has Peterkin Pepit or Dr. Dottle. I had hoped to learn something about the area from another friend, a retired admiral USN, who has been everywhere. All I learned from him was the quality and the quantity of belly dancers from the Kra Isthmus to Singapore. The odd part of it is that he really enjoys good food. One wonders what he does with his spare time.

I do not believe that my naval friend has ever mentioned it, but one of the well-known facts pertaining to seafaring men is that almost all of them plan eventually to retire as far as possible from the sea and run farms. One cannot get very far from the sea on the Malay Peninsula, but practically all of the men in the area are seafaring. After eating this delicious soup, one suspects that all of the retired seafarers turned their hands to raising chickens.

Made traditionally as described under II, this soup requires approximately two hours and a half to make. It is well worth the time. However, it can be done much more quickly in a matter of forty-five minutes as described immediately under I.

I. Malay Chicken Soup (*Quick Version*)

(*Serves 4*)

1 medium onion
3 tablespoons vegetable oil
6 cups chicken stock
½ tablespoon ground cardamon
½ tablespoon ground mace
½ tablespoon monosodium glutamate
1 cup raw rice
2 jars or cans cooked chicken (12 oz. each)
salt
white pepper

Peel and cut onion coarsely. Place oil in a skillet and brown the onion. While onion is browning, place chicken stock in a saucepan. Add the cardamon, mace, and monosodium glutamate. Bring to a boil. Put in the rice. Cover and simmer until the rice is done, approximately twenty-five minutes. Chop the chicken and set aside. When the onions are brown, remove from skillet and drain. When the rice is cooked, add the chopped chicken, stir, taste, and correct seasoning with salt and white pepper as needed. Bring contents of saucepan to a boil. Add the cooked onions. Stir and serve.

II. Malay Chicken Soup (*Traditional Version*)

(*Serves 4*)

2 medium onions
1 carrot
4 sprigs parsley
½ tablespoon ground cardamon
½ tablespoon ground mace
salt
2 celery tops
1 four-pound chicken, cut up
3 tablespoons Wesson oil
1 cup raw rice

Peel one onion and cut into eighths. Scrape carrot and chop very coarsely. Place eight cups water in a large saucepan. Add onion, carrot, parsley, cardamon, mace, salt, and celery tops. Bring to a boil. Add chicken, cover, and simmer for one hour. While chicken is simmering, peel and chop the remaining onion coarsely. Place oil in skillet and brown onion. When chicken is done, drain through a colander, discard vegetables, and reserve stock. Allow chicken to cool enough to handle. Remove all skin, gristle, and bones from the chicken, and chop it into large dice. Wash rice thoroughly in running water. Skim fat from chicken stock. Return stock to saucepan. Bring to a boil. Add rice. Cover, and simmer until done, approximately twenty-five minutes. Add diced chicken and cooked onion. Stir and heat through.

SUGGESTED MENU

With the rice, no bread, of course, is needed or will be desired. Although it does not come from Malaya, an excellent accompaniment to this dish is cucumber and endive salad with French dressing (G). If you feel it needful to serve an alcoholic beverage, why not start the meal with Pimm's No. One Cup or, if you prefer, sake served either chilled or hot?

UWO DANGE NO SHIRU
(Fish-ball Soup)
(*Serves 4*)

The two basic soup stocks in Japanese cooking are "miso" and "dashi." The latter is used primarily for soups which contain fish or seafood. It is made as follows: Boil kelp in the proper quantity of water and as soon as it has come to a hard boil, remove kelp and discard it. Add bonito shavings which have been cut into half-inch squares, a small quantity of monosodium glutamate, and a moderate amount of fish shoyu sauce (G). The saucepan is returned to the fire and boiled until the bonito shavings have fallen to the bottom. The strained liquid is dashi. Dashi is made with dried kelp and dried bonito in the United States, as well as in its native Japan. A simpler process is to use a commercial product that combines the two ingredients in a single small porous bag, each of which miraculously makes three cups of dashi.

An imitation dashi, which is extremely quick and which tastes, curiously enough, more like the original than the suggestions given above, can be made by combining equal parts of bottled clam juice and concentrated beef broth. It is on that basis that the following soup dish is prepared. Incidentally, I should note, perhaps, that neither Pepit or Dr. Dottle has been consulted in this matter. They are unfamiliar with Japan but as both are inveterate cavilers, I am confident they would find something to cavil at in this dish. I did not, and you will not. The quantities given below are ample for four very hungry people. Actually, the soup would probably serve six.

- ½ package frozen, chopped spinach (5 oz. total)
- 1 pound fillet of flounder
- ¾ pound green shrimp
- 3 scallions
- 1 tablespoon monosodium glutamate
- 1 tablespoon ground ginger, or finely minced ginger root
- ¼ tablespoon black pepper
- 2 tablespoons fish shoyu sauce (G)
- ½ tablespoon cornstarch
- 1 tablespoon vegetable oil
- 3 cups clam juice
- 3 cups beef stock
- ½ cup sake

Thaw the spinach. Cut the flounder into strips about an inch wide. Shell and clean the shrimp. Chop the scallions into half-inch pieces. Put all of these ingredients except spinach through a meat grinder, alternating them and using the finest blade. Place ground ingredients in a bowl. Add monosodium glutamate, ginger, pepper, shoyu sauce, cornstarch, and vegetable oil, and work the ingredients into a solid mass with your fingers. Place the clam juice and beef stock in a large saucepan. While they are heating over a low fire, form the ingredients of the bowl into small balls not more than three-fourths of an inch in diameter. When the liquid in the saucepan has come to a boil, gradually drop in the fish balls, being careful not to break them, and add the thawed spinach and sake. Cook gently for ten minutes. The soup is now ready to be served.

SUGGESTED MENU

Like the Chinese, the Japanese serve egg rolls. They make an extremely good opening to a meal and eliminate the need for bread. A good salad for this soup would be made of iceberg lettuce, romaine, chicory, endive and cherry tomatoes. French dressing with mustard of course. I would serve it under an alias and call it a "Kamikaze" Salad. The drink should be either tea or hot sake.

TOHEROA
(Barnacle Soup)
(Serves 4)

Whereas I have never been in New Zealand; and . . .

Whereas none of my culinary friends has visited the Antipodes; and . . .

Whereas New Zealand has a cultural tradition of its own, I, therefore, resolved to request help from the New Zealand Embassy (Washington, D.C., 20008) . . .

My request for assistance was answered by a very charming voice which said substantially: "Oh, yes, we have a very fine soup indeed. It is called 'Toheroa.' Unfortunately, the main ingredient, a kind of barnacle, is not imported into the United States."

After my sigh of disappointment, the voice at the other end of the line relented and said, "Well, you can make almost the same thing with mussels. The chief difference would be in the color. Toheroa Soup is green."

"Fine," said I. "All I have to do is find the mussels and color them with spinach."

The very pleasant voice replied, "Yes, that would work extremely well. Perhaps the spinach would change the taste of the mussels to that of the Toheroa clam."

She very kindly offered to supply me with the recipe for making the soup. I have added the spinach for the color. The only problem still remaining was to find the mussels. These grow abundantly along the East Coast of the United States and yet, for some reason which passeth human understanding, they are almost impossible to find in stores or markets. Fortunately, however, some European countries export to the United States canned mussels already cooked and of a fine quality. It is on the basis of these that this recipe is built. If fresh mussels are available, they certainly should be used. If you use fresh mussels, they should be chopped into small pieces and cooked for five minutes in the stock along with the spinach. In this case, the only garnish will be paprika.

¼ pound spinach
3 cups fish stock
4 tablespoons butter
4 tablespoons sifted flour
1 pint milk
salt
pepper
2 cans mussels (8 oz. each)
paprika

Wash spinach thoroughly. Remove stems and chop leaves fine. Place fish stock in a saucepan. Add spinach. Cover, and cook very hard for five minutes. Melt butter in another saucepan. Add flour and make a roux (G). Heat milk. When roux is cooked, slowly add enough milk to make a thick sauce. Season with salt and pepper. Taste. Set aside eight mussels. Place the remainder in the soup and stir. Mix one-half the contents of each saucepan. Place in a blender and blend at moderate speed for thirty seconds. Repeat with the remainder of the soup and the stock. Combine the two blendings and heat over a moderate fire until the soup is hot through. If the consistency is too thick, thin with milk. Serve very hot in soup plates, each garnished with two of the reserved mussels and sprinkled with one-half teaspoon paprika.

SUGGESTED MENU

It is a long way from the Waitemata River to the Chesapeake Bay, but the ideal bread with Toheroa Soup is Maryland Beaten Biscuit (G). Thus, we draw the world together link by link from Auckland to Baltimore and back. To pull the world even closer together, the ideal salad to accompany this soup is mixed green salad composed of various kinds of lettuces, and French dressing (G). While a great deal of wine is produced in the Antipodes, most of it is similar to that which comes out of California. So, adding another link, it is suggested that the wine be Almadén Mountain White Chablis.

VI

LATIN AMERICA

THE BISHOP'S CALLALOO

(Serves 6)

I met the "Bishop"—neither Episcopal nor chess—through Peterkin Pepit, who had been fortunate enough to meet that charming woman on one of his visits to the Caribbean. I never got to know her as well as I should have liked, but I am indebted to her for several recipes and suggestions. Probably the most interesting of the recipes is what amounts to the national soup of Trinidad and is called Callaloo. This is basically a peasant dish and, as has been noted several times in this connection, filling, wholesome, and good.

Several of the ingredients called for are not available in the United States, and with the Bishop's "ghostly" aid we worked out the recipe based on material available here. While she had eaten Callaloo in Port-of-Spain, she had never made it. She tells me that this Americanized version is very similar to that made in Trinidad.

For those who wish to attempt the recipe as it was originally published in a Trinidad newspaper, it is reproduced under Callaloo II. Land crabs, to which this recipe refers, might be got—if anybody wants them—but dasheen leaves are quite impossible to obtain fresh. Of course, one should (or can) always try.

I. The Bishop's Callaloo (*Quick Version*)

(*Serves* 6)

12 ounces spinach
1 pound okra
1 pound raw corned beef
1 teaspoon chopped chives
8 sprigs parsley
1 teaspoon thyme
4 cloves garlic
1 hot red pepper
¼ teaspoon Angostura Bitters
1 pound crab meat
1 cup coconut milk

Wash spinach thoroughly, remove leaves from stalks, and cut stalks into one-inch lengths. Square off ends of okra and cut into half-inch pieces. Remove as much fat as possible from the corned beef and chop the remaining meat into three-quarter-inch cubes. Place the spinach stalks and leaves, the okra, and the corned beef in a large saucepan or soup kettle and add three quarts water. While water is coming to a boil, chop the chives and remove the leaves from the parsley. Place the chives, the parsley leaves, and the thyme in the soup kettle. Mince the garlic or put it through a press, and add it. Put in the whole red pepper and the Angostura Bitters. When the water comes to a boil, reduce heat, cover, and simmer for thirty-five minutes. Stir from time to time and be sure that the red pepper is not likely to burst; if it reaches the bursting point remove at once. At the end of thirty-five minutes, remove the red pepper anyway, and discard. Add the crabmeat and cook five minutes longer. Put in coconut milk. Cook another three minutes and the soup is ready to serve.

II. The Bishop's Callaloo (*Traditional Version*)

(*Serves* 6)

2 crabs
12 dasheen leaves (the usual bundle from the market)
18 ochroes
some pieces of salt meat, salt beef or the end of a ham bone
chives, thyme, and parsley
2 cloves garlic
½ cup coconut cream made from grated coconut (optional)
(This is optional as it gives the soup a slightly sweet taste which some like. To make it, grate half of a dry coconut. Put into a cloth and place into a bowl. Pour half a pint of boiling water over it. Squeeze in the cloth until all the juice is extracted.)

"Buy the crabs about three days before they are going to be used. Keep them during that period in a pitch oil pan out of which they cannot climb, and feed them on water grass if possible, or ordinary grass cuttings. Put in a branch of a hot pepper bush, at which they will pick. This is to give them a purge, as crabs are foul eaters and if taken straight from the ground to the pot, they do not taste very nice. Leave them a little water in the bottom of the pan too.

"When ready to use, plunge them alive into boiling water and leave for five minutes. Then break off the legs, open up the shell and be especially careful to look for the little black sac in the stomach, part of which is very unpleasant to taste—like the gall of a liver.

"Strip the stalks of the dasheen and remove the mid-ribs. Make the leaves into long rolls and tie into a knot. Break the stalks into inch lengths. Cut the ochroes into small pieces. Put into boiling water with all the seasonings, the salt meat and the crabs.

"Simmer for about three-quarters of an hour. Then swizzle thoroughly with a stick until the ochroes and dasheen are well mixed.

"For those who like it, a hot pepper can be included and removed before serving, but it should not be allowed to cook so much as to break. The coconut juice, if used, should be added at the last minute. The crabs and salt meat can be served on a separate dish, or in the soup as desired. Some like to remove the crab meat from the shells, but mostly it is left in the soup as it is."

SUGGESTED MENU

Almost any variety of bread may be served with this soup. One may also serve rice with it. This has a tendency, however, to make the soup too thick. Hard rolls would be an excellent selection. Inasmuch as New Orleans is not unreasonably far from Port-of-Spain, the delights of Pontalba Salad (G) may have reached the latter city. In any case, it goes well with this soup. No wine is made and little is drunk in Trinidad. To replace it, good rum from the Windward Islands should be served with the coffee.

PUMPKIN SOUP GRENADA

(*Serves 4*)

Another of the Bishop's blessings is this pumpkin soup from the Caribbean. She first cooked it for Pepit. While pumpkins are not noted as an important crop in Grenada, the ways of the Bishop are passing strange. Perhaps she had her own pumpkin patch hard by her residency near Saint George. I have long suspected, with no proof whatever, that she imported already cooked pumpkin in cans. Be that as it may, and that is the way it is going to be, what she did with the pumpkin passeth human understanding, but not human appetite. I well remember saying to Pepit, when he was telling me about the soup: "Heavens above [that was before the days of space walks], man, you can't make soup from a pumpkin any more than you can make a silk purse . . ."

"Cliché!" cried Peterkin triumphantly. "You owe me a guinea." Typically he never dealt in pounds.

". . . out of Dacron," I replied. "*You* now owe *me* two guineas. Pumpkins are for children on All Hallows' Eve and for a kind of confection, which I am sure you have never tasted, called 'punkin pie.' "

"Can the palaver," ses he, "come eat the soup."

I did and, as usual, he was right.

The Bishop had struck again.

The recipe below, as made by the Bishop, calls for already cooked pumpkin and takes about an hour. Her recipe follows as I. If you wish to start with fresh pumpkin, you will add about an hour or more to the cooking time. The result really does not justify the extra time and effort.

I. Pumpkin Soup Grenada (*Quick Version*)

(*Serves 4*)

4 small tomatoes
2 medium onions
2 medium carrots
1 green pepper
3 tablespoons bacon drippings
2 teaspoons minced chives
4 teaspoons minced parsley
3 pints chicken stock
1 teaspoon dill weed
1 teaspoon powdered cinnamon
1 teaspoon powdered ginger
1 teaspoon powdered nutmeg
2 bay leaves
1 can cooked pumpkin meat (32 oz.)
1 teaspoon salt
1½ teaspoons freshly ground pepper
milk
4 tablespoons Barbados rum

Skin tomatoes and onions, scrape carrots, and clean green pepper of seeds and membranes. Chop all vegetables small. Place bacon drippings in a large, heavy saucepan and melt over a moderate flame. Add vegetables and sauté about five minutes. Add to saucepan. Add chicken stock, dill weed, cinnamon, ginger, nutmeg, and bay leaves, and simmer for thirty minutes. Place in blender and agitate at moderate speed for twenty seconds. Put contents of blender through kitchen strainer, discarding contents of strainer. Return soup to fire. Add pumpkin meat, salt, and pepper.

Bring slowly to a boil. If too thick, add milk to thin to desired consistency. Taste and correct seasoning. Just before serving, add rum.

II. Pumpkin Soup Grenada (*Traditional Version*)

(*Serves 4*)

For making the soup with fresh pumpkin the list of ingredients is the same as above except for the substitution of cooked fresh pumpkin for the canned, and except for the actual cooking of the pumpkin the procedure is the same.

Cut a ten-pound pumpkin in half and remove the seeds and membranes as you would with a cantaloupe. Place the pumpkin cut side down in a preheated, moderate oven (325 degrees) and bake it about an hour if it's smaller than ten pounds. A pumpkin large enough to provide two pounds of cooked meat will probably take about an hour and a half. When the pumpkin starts to disintegrate, remove from oven, allow to cool, and then scrape all the meat from the shell. Put the meat into a blender. Add sufficient milk to operate the machine, and run it at moderate speed about thirty seconds or until you have a thick purée. You now proceed to make the soup as previously described.

SUGGESTED MENU

French or Spanish bread goes extremely well with this soup as do various kinds of crackers. For salad, Hazel's Herbage (G) is suggested. Wine is not produced in the Caribbean area although Chile, Brazil, and the Argentine export excellent wines, both red and white, which might be considered with the Pumpkin Soup. The Bishop recommends instead, however, that rum be served with the coffee. She is very fond of rum. So am I.

SOPA DE MAÍZ

(Corn Soup)

(*Serves 4*)

Once again the Bishop rears her lovely head. Somehow she always seems to get involved with dishes from the Caribbean area. This time she was on the consuming rather than the producing end. She pronounced the soup fit for a Carib and that is high praise —from her. How it would be received in Acapulco I have no idea, nor do I care. Where I have eaten it, it is fine indeed. While Sopa de Maíz has some relation to so-called "chowder" made from corn, it is, in my opinion, a superior soup. Most chowders, whether proper fish or seafood soups, as they should be, or bastard varieties, contain potatoes and other ingredients likely to conceal the delicate taste of corn. This recipe allows the pure taste of the maize to come through. While a dozen ears of corn may seem to be more than four people can consume, especially when combined with other food, you will have little soup left over. A reasonably hungry man can eat three ears of corn with no difficulty at all. Try and see for yourself. But the important thing here is that the Bishop liked it. What is good enough for the Bishop is, or should be, good enough for anyone. This soup can be prepared well within the hour of allotted time.

12 ears sweet corn
6 tablespoons tomato paste
1 medium onion
2 tablespoons butter
1 teaspoon salt
1 teaspoon pepper
1 teaspoon chili powder
6 cups milk
12 sprigs parsley
1 gill heavy cream, whipped

Cut the kernels from the cob. Mix tomato paste with six tablespoons water. Slice onion thin. Place butter in a skillet. Add tomato paste mixture, the onion, half of the corn, the salt, pepper, and chili powder. Cook over a medium flame, stirring from time to time, until onions are very soft, about ten minutes. Meanwhile, put the milk into a large saucepan. Add the remaining corn and heat slowly over a low fire for about ten minutes; do not allow it to simmer. While corn cooks, mince parsley. When contents of the skillet are done, add to the contents of the saucepan, stir, and taste. Correct seasoning with salt, pepper, and chili powder to taste. Heat through and serve garnished with a little minced parsley.

This makes a very good cold soup. Place in the refrigerator long enough to chill well, and serve with a tablespoon of unsweetened whipped cream on top.

SUGGESTED MENU

In view of the soup's origin, the proper bread to accompany it is obviously *tostadas* (toasted tortillas). But they, too, are made of corn, and one can have too much of even a good thing. If bread is omitted entirely, I doubt it will be missed. If bread you must have, hard club rolls would suffice. An avocado salad, such as Salad Pontalba (G), would be an excellent choice to follow the soup. No wine comes from Mexico, but good beer does. A few shots of tequila to start the meal and beer with it should put you and your guests in the spirit of the soup, or under the table.

TAPIOCA TOMATO SOUP

(*Serves 4*)

When I was a small boy and going to a school which provided lunch for the pupils, one of the standard and least popular desserts was tapioca pudding. As is probably the case with most young students, it was usually referred to in terms of disgust as "fish eyes." From that time until recently, I was of the firm opinion that tapioca should be properly cooked, prepared, and thrown out the window. This Latin American soup has not completely altered my opinion but it has convinced me that a dish which is edible can be made with tapioca and that it does not require immediate or ultimate defenestration.

My mentor in Latin American cookery shared my opinion of tapioca but also agreed that this soup has very considerable merit. That our original failure to appreciate the merits of tapioca was not remarkable is indicated by the O.E.D. According to that authority, "tapioca," made of words from the Portuguese, the Spanish, and the French, literally means "dregs which have been squeezed out." Despite this graphic description of tapioca, this recipe proves that it can be an important ingredient in a very good soup.

¾ pound veal
1 large onion
1½ tablespoons butter
large bouquet garni (G)
  (2 stalks celery
  1 medium leek
  1 large tomato
  3 sprigs parsley
  8 peppercorns)
1 quart chicken stock
1 slice smoked ham ¼ inch thick
¼ cup tapioca
1 tablespoon chili powder
salt

Remove bone, gristle, and fat from veal and cut it into half-inch cubes. Chop the onion coarsely. Place butter in a heavy saucepan and brown veal and onion in it over a moderate flame. Meanwhile, chop the celery, the leek, the tomato, and the parsley, and add to them peppercorns to make a bouquet garni. When the veal and the onions are brown, add the chicken stock to the saucepan. Put in the bouquet garni. Bring to a boil, cover, and let simmer for thirty minutes. Dice the ham, and add the water, tapioca, and chili powder. Stir well and cook twenty minutes longer. Remove bouquet garni. Taste, and correct the seasoning with salt or additional chili powder.

SUGGESTED MENU

Black bread is probably the best form of starch to accompany this soup. It could well be followed by a simple green salad. One good wine for this meal is a well-chilled California red called Tavola.

SOPA PAN AMERICANA

(*Serves 4*)

Of all the soups in this book, Sopa Pan Americana is undoubtedly the quickest. The story goes, as stories do, that this was an emergency situation in which Peterkin Pepit, or Dr. Dottle—I am not sure which—found himself about to entertain for lunch on very short notice. The entertainer, whatever may have been his plans, was compelled by the fell force of circumstance to have a soup ready in less than an hour. Carefully examining his larder, Pepit (or was it Dottle?) was struck by inspiration and invented this extremely good dish.

While eating it, the guest—a coffee taster—observed more or less as follows:

"Ah, yes, an excellent composite of South American soups. A little too highly seasoned with black pepper, perhaps. I think you have rather more tomato than you need, but after all you were only trying to get the color of Aztec human sacrifice. Still, I should go slow on color in favor of the taste. And, while I am on the subject, I think you were very clever to have included that Irish soup to bring in the O'Haras and Cochranes who worked so hard in the wars of liberation. And that subtle nuance of chicken could come only from the fowl that died in the cock pits of Puerto Rico. How I miss them! And the barley, of course, derives from the sheepherders of Patagonia. Surely that is a Chilean Riesling that you have used."

Coffee tasters must have remarkable palates. The following recipe is the one used by Pepit, or was it Dottle? A longer method can be devised by combining various other soups whose recipes appear in this book. But why bother? The guest was happy and so was the host, naturally. If you want a longer way, why not arrange it yourself? No book is the worse for a little do-it-yourself puzzle (vide *Tristram Shandy*).

- 2 cans concentrated Cream of Chicken Soup (10 oz. each)
- 2 cans Cock-a-Leekie Soup (10 oz. each)
- 1 can Cream of Tomato Soup (10 oz. each)
- ½ cup dry white wine
- ½ teaspoon Scotch Bonnet (G)
- ½ teaspoon freshly ground black pepper
- small croutons (G)

Place the Chicken Soup in the top half of a double boiler. Gradually add the Cock-a-Leekie soup to the container and stir the two together thoroughly with a wooden spoon or wire whisk. When the soups are thoroughly blended, stir in the Tomato Soup, add the white wine, the Scotch Bonnet, and the pepper. Blend thoroughly and heat over boiling water until the soup is hot through. It is now ready to serve. Each diner should be provided with a small saucer of croutons to dunk into the soup as he sees fit.

SUGGESTED MENU

With the barley and the croutons, bread should definitely not be served. An avocado salad, although somewhat rich, would make a good accompaniment to the soup. Serve the same wine that is used in making the soup itself.

SOPA ALBÓNDIGAS
(Meatball Soup)
(*Serves 4*)

This Latin American dish is one of the few included in this book for which there are two short versions. The first one can be done in about twenty minutes, the second one in less than an hour. While either recipe makes an excellent lunch, the speed with which the soup can be put together makes it most suitable for suppers. It is a good suggestion for after-theatre meals. Its best use, however, is to feed those reluctant-to-go-home guests after cocktail parties. They are invited from five-thirty to nine. At ten-thirty or eleven they are still there. You are hungry and, if you eat, you must, alas, feed your guests, too. The quick version, assuming you have the necessary ingredients, is the perfect answer to this problem.

Its effectiveness in overcoming an overindulgence in alcohol is not so great as that of Sauerkraut Soup or so widespread as that of French Onion Soup but it will suffice. It has one great merit unpossessed by the other two; either version may be made very quickly. For those who have the additional half hour to prepare this soup—you probably cannot get overtime pay but you should because the result is worth it—follow No. II.

I. Sopa Albóndigas (*Quick Version*)

(*Serves 4*)

3 small green chili peppers
1 clove garlic
⅓ cup chili sauce
2 eggs
4 sprigs parsley
5 cans Campbell's Beef Broth (10 oz. each)
½ cup dry red wine
2 cans S. S. Pierce cocktail meatballs (6 oz. each)

Remove and discard seeds of peppers and mince very fine. Mince garlic or put through a press. Place the chili sauce in a bowl and mix it well with the other two ingredients. Beat the eggs without mercy and add them to the mixture. Mince the parsley. Add it to the bowl along with one can Beef Broth. Stir everything well. Place the remaining beef broth in a saucepan. Add the wine and bring to a boil. Reduce to a simmer. Add contents of the bowl and the meatballs. Cover the saucepan. Simmer five minutes more and serve.

II. Sopa Albóndigas (*Traditional Version*)

(*Serves 4*)

4 small hot green peppers
¾ pound ground beef
¼ pound ground pork
1 clove garlic
1 teaspoon salt
¼ cup chili sauce
parsley
½ cup bread crumbs (commercial)
2 eggs
3 tablespoons butter
3 pints rich beef stock
½ cup red wine

Remove seeds from peppers and mince small. Put meat (beef and pork) into a mixing bowl. Add minced green peppers to meat. Mince garlic or put through a press and add to bowl. Add salt and chili sauce. Mince enough parsley to make one tablespoon and add to mixture along with bread crumbs. Beat eggs thoroughly and add to bowl, using your fingers, which you will have washed previously. Mix the contents of the bowl thoroughly. Meanwhile, place butter in a skillet and melt. Form the meat and the other ingredients into forty-eight small balls, about three-fourths of an inch in diameter. When the butter is hot, fry the meatballs a few at a time quickly on all sides. While browning the meat, place the beef stock and the wine in a large saucepan and bring to a boil. Add the meatballs and simmer gently for twenty minutes.

SUGGESTED MENU

The best salad to go with this soup is cold artichokes with Vinaigrette dressing (G). This may be served before the soup, with it, or afterward. If the meal is to be served as suggested in the opening paragraphs, to follow a cocktail party, the chances are you will not have cooked cold artichokes in the refrigerator. In that event, a mixed green salad is an obvious substitute. Crusty club rolls should be considered as bread. If you want wine with it, use the same red variety that was used in the soup.

CRISTOBAL STEW

(*Serves 4*)

I never think of Panama without recalling a trip on a banana boat. She was commanded by a wonderful Scot who wrote boys' books, had a magnificent sense of humor, was a lieutenant commander in the United States Naval Reserve, and, perhaps more important, an admiral in the Wisconsin Navy. It seems that on one of the trips from New York to Guatemala some years earlier, he had a female passenger on board who asked him how the chef managed to get fresh milk while at sea.

"Sea cows, madame," said the captain, "sea cows. Every other day we heave to and milk the sea cows so our passengers have fresh milk."

She expressed some skepticism about the story. Two days later while the officers and passengers were having breakfast, the vessel did heave to. There was much movement on the deck above. Chains clanked, a winch was started. The captain said, "Ah, a sea cow." The delay was relatively short and the vessel soon proceeded on its way. One of the crew came down the ladder carying a large, round white object which he presented to the captain.

"Here is the sea cow's egg which you wanted, sir." The captain dutifully presented the egg with an appropriate speech to the doubting female passenger. In the sequel, as the captain passed through the customs shed on his return to New York, he heard the passenger explaining to the customs' officers that she should be permitted to bring the sea cow's egg into the United States duty free because it was an antique. The fact that this story is true is demonstrated by its complete incredibility. What the captain had actually done was to have the cook shave off the outer skin of a coconut and paint the nut with white enamel.

The only connection between that voyage and this soup is bananas. The recipe below calls for the use of green bananas. It may be possible to prepare the recipe in less than two and a half or three hours, but if the soup is to be at its best, it should be made at least twenty-four hours before it is served, and preferably two days. The extra time permits the soup to mellow, and to thicken slightly. From that point of view, it is, therefore, a quick soup, as it need only be heated and served.

1 slice ham, ¼ inch thick
¾ pound top round of beef
1½ pounds lean pork
1 large clove garlic
2 teaspoons salt
1 bay leaf
3 scallions
2 limes
2 yellow squash
2 medium potatoes
¾ pound Polish sausage
½ teaspoon curry powder
½ teaspoon cayenne pepper
½ teaspoon ground cloves
2 green bananas

Remove and discard all fat from the ham, the beef, and the pork. Dice ham and cut beef and pork into one-inch cubes. Place meat in a large saucepan. Add four cups water and heat over a low flame. While water is coming to a boil, peel and mince the garlic or put through a press. Add garlic, salt, and bay leaf to the saucepan. Cover, and simmer until the meat is tender, approximately an hour and a half. While the saucepan simmers, mince the scallions. Squeeze limes, reserving the juice. Wash, peel and cube the squash. Peel and dice the potatoes. Cut the sausage into one-fourth-inch rounds. When the meat is done, add scallions, lime juice, squash, potatoes, sausage, curry powder, cayenne pepper, and cloves. Cover, and continue to cook for another twenty minutes. Meanwhile, cut the bananas into half-inch slices. Add them to the stew and cook ten minutes longer. The soup may be served now but, as mentioned elsewhere, it is much better if allowed to stand for at least twenty-four hours. To this end, it should be put into a mixing bowl, covered, and put into the refrigerator until needed.

SUGGESTED MENU

Any crusty bread or hard club rolls go well with the soup. The ideal salad, of course, would be a hard-cooked sea cow's egg appropriately chopped and delicately arranged on a bed of lettuce and dressed with mayonnaise. This is an impractical suggestion. Why not substitute some thinly sliced tomatoes and cucumbers, also tastefully arranged on a bed of lettuce, and dressed with oil, vinegar, salt, and pepper. This dish practically screams for rosé wine. Tavel would be a good choice.

AZTEC SHRIMP SOUP

(*Serves 4*)

It is well known that the Soldan of Byzantium and his Saracen predecessors were wont to astonish their dinner guests by serving them cold sherbet made with snow from the mountains and carried to the palace by relays of couriers. Byzantium was not the only country which used that method to provide rare and fresh food for the table. The halls of Montezuma, scores of miles from the sea, offered fresh seafood brought to the emperor's kitchens by runners. Both the Pacific Ocean and the Gulf of Mexico abound in fish and crustacea of all kinds. When Cortez and his followers first arrived in Mexico, the Aztecs treated them with deference and hospitality. It must have come as a great and pleasant surprise to the Spaniards to eat, so far from salt water, fresh food which reminded them of that from their own Mediterranean. Eventually, of course, parts of the Mexican cuisine were merged with that of Spain so that today much of the so-called Mexican food served in the United States, particularly in the Southwest, is derived from this merger. This soup, which is based in a rather offhand way on an old Aztec recipe, requires comparatively little time to prepare. It is quite filling, and if properly sprinkled with chili powder warms the cockles and muscles of the heart. It makes a splendid luncheon on a raw, rather wet fall day. It is equally good in the winter, spring, or summer.

While making Aztec Shrimp Soup is by no means a full day's work, a much more rapid version is possible if you use prepared foods. So, if you begrudge the time to make the traditional version, this recipe will allow you to feed your guests extremely well in well under an hour. For those with time and a desire to eat the soup as it was made—possibly—in Montezuma's kitchens the traditional version appears as II.

I. Aztec Shrimp Soup (*Quick Version*)

(*Serves 4*)

1 tablespoon lemon juice
1 pound green shrimp
1 small can tomato paste (6 oz.)
1 medium yellow onion
3 tablespoons olive oil
1 can small whole white potatoes (16 oz.)
2 teaspoons orégano
1 teaspoon garlic powder
chili powder

Put two quarts water in a large saucepan. Add lemon juice, bring to a boil, put in shrimp. Cover, and simmer for five minutes. At the end of that time, remove shrimp, reserving liquid, and allow shrimp to cool. Meanwhile, mix tomato paste with double the amount of water. Peel and dice onion coarsely. Place olive oil in a small skillet, and cook onion until soft but not brown. Drain potatoes, discarding liquid, and cut potatoes into half-inch cubes. By now shrimp will be cool enough to handle. Shell them and cut into bite-size pieces. Put tomato paste mixture, potato cubes, chopped shrimp, and contents of small skillet into reserved liquid in saucepan. Add orégano, garlic powder, and one tablespoon chili powder. Stir well, and bring to a boil. Remove from fire, and skim off fat. Taste, and correct seasoning with salt and pepper as required. Return to fire, heat through, and season each serving with a sprinkling of chili powder.

II. Aztec Shrimp Soup (*Traditional Version*)

(*Serves 4*)

1 tablespoon lemon juice
1 pound green shrimp
1 medium yellow onion
2 medium tomatoes
1 pound very small potatoes
2 teaspoons orégano
1 teaspoon salt
½ teaspoon freshly ground black pepper
3 tablespoons olive oil
2 small cloves garlic
chili powder

Place two quarts water in a large saucepan or soup kettle. Add lemon juice, bring to a boil, put in shrimp and boil slowly for five minutes. At the end of that time, remove shrimp, reserving liquid, and allow to cool enough to be shelled. While shrimp are cooking and cooling, peel and chop the onion into coarse dice. Skin the tomatoes, and remove seeds. Cut tomatoes into pieces about an inch square. Peel the potatoes and cut them into half-inch pieces. Shell shrimp and return to saucepan or kettle; add tomatoes and potatoes. Sprinkle with orégano, salt, and pepper. Cover and simmer fifteen minutes. Meanwhile put olive oil in a small skillet or heavy saucepan. Heat and add chopped onion and the garlic, put through a press or minced very fine. Cook over low heat until onion and garlic are soft but not brown. At the end of the fifteen minutes add to saucepan contents of skillet and one tablespoon chili powder. Cover, and simmer thirty minutes. Allow soup to cool sufficiently to skim off fat. Reheat thoroughly but do not cook. Taste, correct seasoning with salt or pepper. Place in soup plates, sprinkle each plate with a bit of chili powder, and serve.

SUGGESTED MENU

In view of the soup's origin, the obvious bread is corn sticks, although with the potatoes in the soup no bread is really essential. The salad should be simple and without tomatoes. A mixed green salad is extremely good with the soup or after it. Louis Martini's Mountain Red has the right body and taste to bring out the flavor of the soup itself.

MARISCOS DE VALPARAISO
(Shellfish Stew)
(*Serves* 4)

A highly civilized country whose seacoast extends twenty-six hundred miles roughly from the Tropic of Capricorn to the Horn and whose greatest width is only two hundred twenty miles is likely to include a great deal of seafood and fish in its cuisine. This appealing Chilean soup is only one example of that country's contribution to gastronomy. Before the Germans in World War I began pulling nitrogen out of the air, Chile was one of the most important exporters of this element. This bit of extraneous information is included only for collectors of extraneous information. Fortunately, the source of Chilean nitrogen has nothing whatever to do with Chilean cuisine. The exact origin of this particular dish has not been established nor has it ever been proved that it was one of the favorite seafoods of Bernardo O'Higgins who, despite his somewhat uncertain ancestry, was a benevolent dictator of the country for five years. If, indeed, he had a predilection for this soup, he could have found it during his exile in Peru.

Mariscos de Valparaiso may be made with fish stock or clam juice. The taste is different but who is to say which is better? Obviously, clam juice is the quicker. In either case, the soup can be done in less than an hour.

1 large onion
6 tablespoons butter
6 tablespoons flour
4 cups fish stock (or 3 bottles clam juice, 12 oz. each)
1 bottle Chilean white wine
½ teaspoon white pepper
2 eggs
1 pound green shrimp
1 pound scallops
3 hot chili peppers
½ cup almonds
1 cup heavy cream
1 tablespoon paprika

Chop the onion small. Melt butter in large saucepan and sauté onion until soft and slightly brown. Add flour and make a roux (G). When the roux is cooked, gradually add the fish stock and wine to the saucepan. Add the white pepper. Bring to a boil and simmer covered for thirty minutes. While the contents of the saucepan are simmering, hard-cook the eggs. Peel the green shrimp and cut into one-half-inch pieces. Cut the scallops the same size. Remove seeds from the peppers and mince them. Grind the almonds and chop the eggs small. When contents of saucepan have simmered thirty minutes, add the shrimp, scallops, the hot peppers, and simmer five minutes longer. Put in the ground almonds, eggs, and cream. Heat briefly. Garnish with paprika and serve hot.

SUGGESTED MENU

Tostadas or crackers known as Sea Toast will serve well as bread with this soup. The dish is reasonably heavy and requires a fairly light salad. One made of two or three kinds of lettuce with perhaps a few tomatoes would be admirable. Use a French dressing (G). The wine should be the same as that used in making the soup.

VII

CREOLE COOKERY

COURT BOUILLON CREOLE

(*Serves 4*)

To most gastronomes and chefs, court bouillon is a liquid for poaching fish. It is composed of quantities of wine, water, vinegar, lemon juice, onions, carrots, parsley, celery, and pepper. Few court bouillons contain all of these ingredients. No matter what its composition, a court bouillon is a splendid liquid in which to cook almost any kind of fish or seafood. Court Bouillon Creole, however, is quite literally a different kettle of fish. It is not a liquid intended for cooking fish, but is a fish soup as is made in the bayou country. As with several other soups in this collection, we are all indebted to Mrs. Dorothy Gaston of Bellaire, Texas, of whom you will hear more. You will find this recipe worth your attention.

Creole cookery takes time and no short cuts are possible. The results justify the effort in every instance. One possible but paradoxical short cut for this particular recipe would be to take two days instead of four hours to prepare the dish. To take this "short cut," you follow all the directions down to the introduction of the fish and the filé gumbo (G) into the stock, and refrigerate the stock itself overnight. Approximately forty-five minutes before you wish to serve the soup, remove the stock from the refrigerator, place it over a moderate fire for ten minutes, and then follow the directions as given. Any other method of decreasing the time is likely to have unfortunate results.

2½ pounds red snapper
1¼ teaspoons salt
1 teaspoon freshly ground black pepper
1 medium onion
2 green peppers
4 stalks celery
½ cup bacon drippings
½ can tomato paste (6 oz. can)
1 tablespoon Worcestershire sauce
½ cup white wine
¼ teaspoon cayenne pepper
8 scallions
6 large sprigs parsley
3 bay leaves
1 teaspoon sweet basil
⅛ teaspoon orégano
¼ cup rice
1 tablespoon filé gumbo (G)

Have fish filleted, discarding head. Place bones and tail in large saucepan. Add one and a half cups water, one teaspoon salt, and a half teaspoon black pepper. Cover saucepan and simmer for twenty minutes to make fish stock. Meanwhile, chop fillets into two-inch squares and set aside. Chop onion, green pepper, and celery small. In a large, heavy saucepan, place the bacon drippings, add the chopped onion, green pepper, and celery, and cook over a low flame until soft. Meanwhile, mix tomato paste with an equal part water. Then drain the fish bones, retaining the liquid, and remove any meat adhering to bones, adding it to the chopped fish. Discard bones. When vegetables are soft, add to saucepan the tomato paste mixture, fish stock, Worcestershire sauce, and wine. Add remaining salt, pepper, and cayenne pepper. While vegetables are cooking, chop the scallions small and chop the parsley. Add these, the bay leaves, basil, and orégano to the liquid. Cover, and simmer gently for two hours. While soup is simmering, boil rice. At the end of two hours, add fish squares and simmer hard for twenty minutes. Add filé gumbo. Remove from fire and allow to stand for five minutes. Remove bay leaves; taste, and correct seasoning. Place in each soup dish two tablespoons cooked rice; cover with soup and serve.

SUGGESTED MENU

As with most Creole soups, this one calls for rice. No bread is required. Pontalba Salad (G) is obvious but it is a little too heavy to go with the soup. Perhaps a good substitute would be Old Man Sean's Sallet (G). The wine, naturally, will be white and dry.

SHRIMP GUMBO GASTON

(*Serves* 4)

Gumbos may be made with almost every kind of food: fish, crustacea, fowl, meat, game, or greens alone. Most of them are based on shellfish, probably because shrimp, lobster, crabs, and crayfish abound in Louisiana waters and in the Gulf of Mexico generally. This, the first gumbo in the book, was selected because it is the simplest. Once you have tried this one, the others will follow as the night the day and you cannot then be false to any of them.

Those two great friends, Peterkin Pepit and Dr. Fergus X. Dottle, were wont to make semiannual pilgrimages to New Orleans just to eat gumbos. The first trip was ostensibly to attend a Mardi Gras ball but their friends all knew the real objectives were Galatoire's, Arnaud's, and Antoine's among others. Those restaurants were and still are worth the journey, but you can make excellent gumbos *chez vous.*

Most gumbos made with the same basic ingredients do not vary too much, but Shrimp Gumbo Gaston possesses one unique characteristic: the addition of sweet onion slices and vinegar just before serving. Mrs. Gaston, whose forebears brought the recipe from Louisiana many years ago, was kind enough to share it. I am deeply indebted to her. And so are you.

3 tablespoons sifted flour
1 teaspoon lemon juice
2 pounds green shrimp
2½ tablespoons bacon drippings
½ pound okra
1 medium onion
1 pound tomatoes
1 large clove garlic
¼ pound cooked ham
4½ teaspoons salt
2½ teaspoons freshly ground pepper
2 large sweet white onions
½ cup cider vinegar

Place flour in a cake pan and brown—but do not let burn—in a hot (400 degrees) oven. Place four cups water in a saucepan, add lemon juice, bring to a boil, and toss in shrimp. Cover, bring to a boil, reduce heat and simmer for five minutes. Drain, reserving shrimp and stock. Peel shrimp and cut into bite-size pieces. Put drippings in large, heavy saucepan or soup kettle. Heat over a low flame, add browned flour and make a roux (G). Cook about five minutes, stirring frequently with a wooden spoon. Cut okra into quarter-inch slices. When roux is cooked, add okra, and cook over moderate flame, stirring occasionally, until all gumminess has gone, about ten minutes. While okra is cooking, peel onion, skin tomatoes, and chop both coarsely. When okra is done, add chopped onion, and garlic put through a press or very finely minced. Cook until onion is lightly browned. Meanwhile, dice ham. When onion is brown, add tomatoes, break up with a wooden spoon, and put in diced ham, three teaspoons salt, one and a half teaspoons pepper, and three cups shrimp stock. Cover and simmer three hours. Peel and cut white onions into very thin slices. Place in a bowl, sprinkle with remaining salt and pepper, and cover with the vinegar. Allow to marinate until contents of kettle have simmered two hours and forty-five minutes. Add chopped shrimp to kettle, stir well, and cook fifteen minutes more. When ready to serve, put the gumbo into hot soup plates and add four slices of marinated onion and two tablespoons of the marinade to each plate.

I agree with Mrs. Gaston that this "really makes for licking good eating."

SUGGESTED MENU

Normally a gumbo is served with "plenty of well-dried rice," to quote my gumbo benefactor. Rice certainly may be served with this soup but I prefer French bread. Both may be used, for that matter. The salad should be simple: lettuce and sliced tomatoes. The wine should be light, white, and dry. Any of the Rieslings, either domestic or imported, would be appropriate.

GUMBO Z'HERBES

(*Serves* 6)

Thirteen greens are used to make this soup. It is, or at least was, served in Louisiana about Eastertide, each green supposedly representing one of the diners at the Last Supper. This is legend, but the soup is legendary too, in a different sense. As with most old recipes handed down orally within families, and probably not written down for a century, instructions for preparing Gumbo z'Herbes differ in ingredients, quantities, and results. When oral transmission is complicated by the fact that the recipe derives from three or four different cultures, the final products are not likely to be uniform. This can lead to culinary adventure. The list of greens given below is augmented by another list, any item of which may be substituted for almost any other green in the recipe. Watercress, spinach, lettuce, parsley, and cabbage are the only "untouchables." Actually I think land cress (also sold as garden cress), when available, is preferable to Brussels sprouts. The soup is obviously a very old Creole dish, showing French, Spanish, and African influence. But the odd fact is that by definition it really is not a gumbo. A gumbo must contain okra. This does not. But it is informally called a "gumbo" and may well antedate all other gumbos. The internal evidence indicates, also, that this was a "peasant" dish. All of the greens are inexpensive, easily grown—except endive—and many of them are vegetable tops which were clearly added to the soup pot while the roots themselves were served at another meal. Almost all such peasant dishes are good, wholesome, and filling. Gumbo z'Herbes is no exception.

A note of warning must be appended here. When this soup was prepared in Louisiana kitchens a hundred years ago, kitchen help was no problem. Now you would be well advised to allow yourself a good day to make the soup. It is worth the time. Two people, working steadily, but not at very high speed—naturally drinks had to be made and consumed—required three and a half hours to strip the stems and the heavy ribs from the greens. On no account omit the bacon, it is integral to the dish.

1 bunch broccoli
1 pint Brussels sprouts
1 bunch watercress
1 pound spinach
½ head iceberg lettuce
½ head small cabbage
1 bunch raddish tops
1 bunch turnip tops
1 bunch beet tops
½ pound kale
1 bunch parsley
½ pound mustard greens
½ pound collard greens
3 large leeks
1 pound pickled pork
2 tablespoons lard
2 cloves garlic
4 tablespoons flour
½ teaspoon cayenne pepper
bouquet garni (G)
(6 white peppercorns
½ teaspoon marjoram
7 whole allspice
25–30 fresh sage leaves
1 bay leaf)
2 teaspoons salt
2 tablespoons vinegar
¼ cup raw rice
12 slices bacon
Alternate greens:
1 bunch carrot tops
6 stalks endive
1 bunch chicory
½ pound rape
½ pound land cress
½ pound kohlrabi

Cut flowers from broccoli, and bottoms from sprouts. Discard all stems. Place broccoli flowers and sprout leaves in a large bowl. Remove and discard all stems and thick ribs from other greens, and place the leaves in the same bowl. (You probably will need two bowls.) Wash all greens and vegetables very thoroughly. Then wash them again and place in a large soup kettle, but do not pack them; use two kettles if necessary. Barely cover with water, bring to a boil, and simmer gently for twenty minutes. Meanwhile, cut leeks into small pieces; wash well. Cut pork into large dice. Place lard in a skillet, melt, and add leeks and chopped pork. Put garlic through a press or mince very fine and add to skillet. Cook over a moderate flame until leeks are soft and pork is lightly browned. Add flour and cayenne pepper to make a roux (G). Cook roux about five minutes, stirring constantly. Remove skillet from fire, cover, and set aside.

By now the greens should have had their twenty minutes. Strain them, reserving the liquid. Return liquid to soup kettle, bring to a boil and cook down to five pints. Allow greens to cool enough to handle. While liquid is being reduced and greens cool, make bouquet garni. Now mince the cooked greens very fine, either with a vegetable chopper or a knife. The former is much faster, of course. Do not use a blender or you will have a kind of mush.

Return skillet to fire, and gradually add one pint of hot liquid from the kettle. Stir well over moderate heat to make a kind of thick sauce. Continue to cook, stirring occasionally, until the sauce begins to bubble. Remove liquid from soup kettle, and reserve. Place contents of skillet in the kettle, add the minced greens, stir well. Gradually add the rest of the liquid, and over a moderate flame stir until it reaches a common consistency. Add bouquet garni, salt, and vinegar. Cover kettle and simmer one hour. While soup is simmering boil the rice and sauté the bacon. When bacon is done drain on paper towels, and chop into small pieces. Keep rice warm.

At the end of the hour remove and discard bouquet garni. Taste and correct seasoning. Place one tablespoon cooked rice in each soup plate, fill with soup, and garnish with one half tablespoon chopped bacon. Serve at once. If you prefer to serve from a tureen, place the rice and the chopped bacon in separate warm dishes beside the server and garnish at the table.

SUGGESTED MENU

While it contains some of the same ingredients as the soup, the logical salad would be Pontalba Salad (G). A crusty French bread is ideal with this gumbo. A rosé wine is to be preferred to a red or a white with this dish. Tavel is probably the best-known rosé, but if your wine merchant can get it for you, the Boordy Vineyards at Westminster, Maryland, make, I think, a more suitable wine for drinking with the gumbo. Either will add to the meal's pleasure.

RABBIT GUMBO

(*Serves 4*)

Naturally this recipe for gumbo comes from Louisiana, but in a circuitous way. In 1836 it was carried, along with other goods and chattels, from Bayou La Fourche in Saint Mary's Parish to Houston in the then independent country of Texas. One suspects that it was entrusted to the personal keeping of "Aunt French Mary" the much-loved body servant of Anais Brou who had married Monsieur Bousquet Druzin Folse and went with him to the new nation. The journey was apparently motivated entirely by a spirit of adventure as the couple was fiscally sound, and neither was sought by the law—unusual at the time. The recipe has remained a jealously guarded family secret until now. The great-great-granddaughter (in this case the "grand" could well be separated from "daughter") of M. Folse persuaded his great-grandson to part with it, no small feat.

The original recipe calls for shrimp, but in view of the prevalence of jack rabbits in the country and later, the state, of Texas, I have substituted rabbit for shrimp. I suffered no inconvenience from the change as I had a rabbit but no shrimp. If you want a shrimp gumbo, use the shrimp gumbo recipe.

Before you can make a rabbit gumbo you have to cook a rabbit, a fairly simple culinary process. First you catch your rabbit, which, presumably, you will do at your butcher's. Have him remove the head, skin the animal, clean it, and cut it up as he would a stewing chicken. Be sure the backbone is split into pieces which will fit your largest stew pot. Disjointing a rabbit is no great chore, and you can do it yourself with a sharp knife and the scantiest notion of rabbit anatomy. This recipe is in two parts.

Part One

1 medium onion
1 medium carrot
½ medium turnip
bouquet garni (G)
(½ teaspoon thyme
1 bay leaf
3 small sprigs parsley)
1 three-pound rabbit, cut up
1 teaspoon salt
12 peppercorns
½ lemon

Peel the onion and cut into large pieces. Scrape carrot and peel turnip, chop into three or four pieces each. Make bouquet garni. Put enough water into a large saucepan or kettle to cover the rabbit. Bring the water to a boil, put in the rabbit. When the water starts to boil again add the vegetables, salt, peppercorns, bouquet garni, and the juice from the lemon. Cover and reduce heat so that the water boils very gently. Cook for about fifty minutes. Remove rabbit from broth and set aside to cool. Allow the broth to boil slowly, uncovered, until it has been reduced by about twenty-five percent. Strain into a bowl, discarding the vegetables and bouquet garni. When the rabbit is cool enough to handle, strip the meat from the bones. Discard the bones, and dice the small meat. Set meat and broth aside until needed for the gumbo.

Part Two

- 1 medium onion
- 1 pound tomatoes
- ¾ pound okra
- 1½ tablespoons lard
- 3 tablespoons sifted flour
- 1 clove garlic
- ¾ pound diced rabbit meat
- 4½ cups stock from rabbit (*vide supra*)
- 2 teaspoons salt
- 8 tablespoons cooked rice

Peel and slice onion and tomatoes very fine. Square off ends of okra and cut into quarter-inch slices. Put lard in large skillet, melt, and add flour to make a roux (G); cook, stirring with a wooden spoon, for about five minutes. Add onion slices and cook, turning very frequently with a cake turner or large offset spatula for about seven minutes more or until onion ceases to sizzle. Put in okra and tomatoes, cook, mixing constantly, for another seven minutes, or until okra is no longer sticky. Add garlic through a press. Cook, still turning, for about three minutes. Transfer contents of skillet to a large, heavy saucepan (three-quart capacity) using a small quantity of water if necessary to scrape odds and ends from skillet. Add two cups rabbit stock, cover, and simmer gently for one hour, stirring gently about every fifteen minutes with a wooden spoon. Put in rabbit meat, salt, and remainder of rabbit stock. Cover and continue to simmer for another half hour, stirring twice. Put two tablespoons rice in each of four large hot soup plates. Divide the gumbo among the plates and serve right away.

SUGGESTED MENU

With the rice, bread is not necessary, but if it is desired, French bread is the obvious and best choice. This soup is very hearty indeed and should be followed by a light salad. A mixed green salad would be admirable. For the same reason the meal will support a hearty wine. Burgundy goes well with rabbit; also with rabbit gumbo.

BAYOU OYSTER CHOWDER

(*Serves 4*)

Many of the stories centering around *les frères* Lafitte are myths. Two of these legends are that Pierre Lafitte invented this oyster chowder and that his brother Jean had it served to Andrew Jackson and himself in the Absinthe House as they planned the defense of New Orleans shortly before Sir Edward Pakenham began his advance on the city. If Pierre invented the chowder it is a far, far better thing he did than he had done before. The chowder is a truly noble dish and well suited to an intimate luncheon. Cut the quantities in half for two people and serve champagne, of course. The oyster's reputation for causing certain desirable biologic effects is, alas, undeserved. But, administered under the proper conditions, the chowder might seem to give substance to the oyster's spurious reputation. Whether served to two, or four, or more, the soup will please the palate, gladden the eye, and edify the soul.

Because oysters themselves take very little time to cook, this recipe can be done quickly. If you start out with your eggs already hard-cooked, the soup itself should be made in a maximum of an hour and probably can be done in forty minutes.

2 eggs
2 quarts large oysters
1 large onion
1 medium carrot
3 stalks celery
2 cloves garlic
½ pound butter
5 teaspoons bay leaves, broken
1 teaspoon thyme
2 cups loose fresh parsley leaves
2 scallions
4 tablespoons flour
3 pints milk
salt
freshly ground black pepper
cayenne pepper

Hard-cook eggs and put in refrigerator to cool. Place oysters in a colander over a bowl to drain. Help the draining from time to time by disturbing oysters with a wooden spoon. Reserve the oyster liquor, of course. Peel onion, scrape carrot, and mince both along with celery stalks. Put all together in a small bowl. Mince garlic or put it through a press and add to the bowl. Place four tablespoons butter in a skillet, melt butter, and add contents of bowl, along with broken bay leaves and thyme. Cook over high heat, stirring often, until contents of skillet are dark brown, about fifteen minutes. Add oyster liquor and simmer, covered, for five minutes. Remove from heat and allow to cool. Meanwhile, mince parsley leaves and scallions; set aside. Shell eggs, remove and discard whites, and mince the yolks with a sharp knife. Place remaining butter in a large saucepan, melt, and add flour. Make a roux (G) and cook, stirring constantly to prevent burning, until roux is dark brown; remove from heat. Place contents of skillet in a blender, add one cup milk, and blend at moderate speed for forty seconds. Return roux to stove, and over moderate heat gradually add contents of blender, stirring well all the time, until contents of saucepan begin to simmer. Once milk has been introduced into this recipe, the soup must never be allowed to boil. Remove saucepan from heat, add the minced parsley, scallions, and remainder of milk. Heat over a low fire, and just before liquid comes to a simmer, put in one-half teaspoon salt, one-quarter teaspoon pepper, and one-quarter teaspoon cayenne pepper. Stir well. Taste and correct seasoning. Remember that the effect of the pepper will not be immediately apparent. Add oysters and continue to cook until oysters are just done, that is when they are plump and edges have curled. If overcooked, oysters shrink and become hard. Place chowder in a very hot tureen or in soup plates, garnish with minced egg yolk, and serve. The chowder must be very hot.

SUGGESTED MENU

The best bread to accompany the chowder is commercial: either oysterettes, or Trenton oyster crackers. Salade Flandre (G) is the proper salad. The wine should be a well-chilled Chablis, or champagne (*vide supra*).

ROYAL STREET SHRIMP BISQUE

(*Serves* 2)

There was, but, alas, no longer is, a restaurant on Royal Street in New Orleans called Gluck's. Some aesthetic disagreement existed among its patrons as to the décor and general atmosphere but all agreed that Gluck's Shrimp Bisque was in a class by itself. If it was not the best in the world, it was the best in New Orleans, no small thing in itself. Aside from its delicious flavor and creamlike consistency, it had another unusual claim on the diner's attention: its appearance. Swimming around on the unruffled pink surface of this laudable concoction were the deliciously stuffed heads of some of the shrimp used to make the bisque. Their little beady black eyes gazed unblinkingly at the diner as though trying to convey the hope that he would choke to death on their dead bodies. Regular patrons ignored the eyes: after all no one ever had choked to death on Henry Gluck's Shrimp Bisque. The gaze may have disconcerted newcomers, but those who had the chance usually returned. That soup was an experience—one to be repeated whenever the opportunity offered.

This bisque traditionally requires time and effort. There is a quick version. For those who have an urgent craving for immediate Shrimp Bisque, all is not lost. This version, of course, omits the shrimp heads.

There are a number of canned and frozen Shrimp Bisques on the market, which, while in themselves leaving something to be desired, can be used as a basis for preparing quite a good soup. I prefer Campbell's frozen Cream of Shrimp Soup, probably because I am used to it.

If the time is available and you wish to enjoy the wonders of Mr. Gluck's establishment, try II.

I. Royal Street Shrimp Bisque (*Quick Version*)

(*Serves* 2)

2 cans frozen condensed shrimp soup (10 oz. each)
1 can milk (10 oz.)
½ cup dry sherry
8 small cooked shrimp
½ teaspoon freshly ground pepper
½ teaspoon Pernod
1 cup small croutons (G)

Thaw the frozen soup according to the directions on the container. Place the soup in the top half of a double boiler. Add the milk and sherry. Heat slowly over hot water, stirring occasionally to blend the components smoothly. While the soup is heating, chop the shrimp into half-inch pieces. If they are very small Gulf shrimp, you will not chop them at all. Put the pepper in the soup, which must not be allowed to boil. Add the chopped shrimp, and simmer five minutes. Stir in Pernod. Serve at once, with croutons on the side as below.

II. Royal Street Shrimp Bisque (*Traditional Version*)

(*Serves* 2)

2 cups Velouté Sauce (G)
½ medium onion
½ medium carrot
3 tablespoons butter
2 sprigs parsley
⅛ teaspoon thyme
½ bay leaf
1 cup dry white wine
24 large green shrimp
1 cup milk
½ teaspoon freshly ground pepper
½ teaspoon Pernod
1 cup small croutons (G)

This recipe uses a Velouté Sauce as a liaison or binding agent. It will be well to make that first. In this instance I would substitute clam juice for fish stock in making the sauce; it helps the flavor. When the sauce is finished, cover, and proceed with the recipe.

Chop the onion and carrot into fine dice. Melt two tablespoons butter in a large saucepan. Cook the onion and carrot in the butter over a slow heat. While they are cooking, mince the parsley. Add it, the thyme, and the half bay leaf to the saucepan. Continue to cook slowly until the onion is soft and transparent. Add the wine. When mixture is hot, put in the shrimp, and stir to be sure they are well coated with contents of skillet. Cover the saucepan and simmer the contents very gently for about eight minutes. Remove shrimp, reserving remaining contents, called a *mirepoix.* Peel six shrimp, and add the shells to the remaining shrimp. Cut the six peeled shrimp into half-inch slices and reserve. Chop the rest of the shrimp, including all the shells, as fine as possible. Place these shrimp, shells, *mirepoix,* and one half of the Velouté Sauce in a blender and blend at high speed for thirty seconds. Return contents of the blender to the rest of the sauce. If the contents of the saucepan are now thicker than you like, add as much of the milk as needed to bring them to the desired consistency. Stir well, add pepper, return contents of saucepan to blender. Blend at high speed for another thirty seconds. Place a kitchen strainer over a large mixing bowl. Pour the contents of the blender into the strainer, and, using a wooden spoon, force all the liquid into the bowl. When the contents of the strainer are as dry as you can make them, discard. Return the bisque to the saucepan. You may keep it for several hours; for several days if you refrigerate it. Just before you are ready to serve the bisque, place it over a low heat, add the chopped shrimp, the stuffed shrimp heads if you have made them, the remaining tablespoon butter, and the Pernod. When the bisque is hot through, but before it boils, serve it. Divide the croutons and place half on the right side of each diner.

The preceding recipe, alas, does not include the shrimp heads. In most American cities and towns green shrimp have lost their heads before appearing on the market. Then, too, not everyone wants to take the trouble to make the forcemeat. If you cannot forgo the pleasure of staring back at the little beady eyes of the shrimp as you eat the soup, you prepare the stuffed heads in this manner. In addition to the twenty-four shrimp called for in the recipe, procure eight other large shrimp, complete with heads, of course. Place the eight in rapidly boiling salted water to which the juice of half a lemon has been added. Let them boil about five minutes. Remove from water, drain, and allow to cool. When cool enough to handle, gently break the shrimp about an inch back of the head, and remove all the meat, being careful not to damage the carapace. Remove from the tail portions all the meat and discard the shell. Chop the shrimp meat very fine. Now make a *panade* by combining one-half cup fresh fine bread crumbs with three ounces dry white wine, a little salt, and freshly ground pepper. Add the minced shrimp to this mixture. Put through a blender (high speed for thirty seconds). Put into an ordinary kitchen sieve and press out as much liquid as possible. Discard liquid. Stuff the shrimp carapaces with the forcemeat left in the sieve. Add the stuffed heads to the bisque when it starts its final simmering.

SUGGESTED MENU

While not all Shrimp Bisques come from New Orleans, this one seems to have started there, so we would be wise to select a salad from that city, Pontalba Salad (G). It is rich but not gaudy, and goes well with this bisque. You will need no bread other than the croutons. A light, dry white wine might be offered. While going rather far from New Orleans to get it, you will enjoy a nicely chilled bottle of Soave from Italy.

VIII

HERE AND THERE

SOUP SENEGALESE

(*Serves 4*)

This cold soup from Dakar is highly flavored with curry and recommended for very hot weather. How this admirable condiment indigenous to the East found its way into French West Africa is not clear. France, at one time, was seized of considerable territory in India and it is possible that some Government official, civil or military, transferred from the Coromandel Coast to Dakar, brought curry with him, or his wife with her. No place has a climate better suited to curry than the area along the Senegal River. The soup makes a very good first course for a meal as well as a main course for a light luncheon. It has much merit, too, about eleven o'clock on a hot morning, when the wine has run both red and deep the night before.

While this African soup does not require any great length of time to prepare, it does take time to chill properly. The time can be reduced to an absolute minimum by using cold Vichyssoise as the basis for the soup. If Vichyssoise is placed in the refrigerator, along with the milk, and both are thoroughly chilled, the soup can be eaten almost as soon as it is put together from this simple recipe.

Some of the character of Soup Senegalese is lost in the quick version so that the second and traditional version is recommended. Again, the extra preparation of the ingredients and the soup itself is not time consuming. The chilling is. Version II is best if left in the refrigerator overnight.

I. Soup Senegalese (*Quick Version*)

(*Serves* 4)

4 cans chilled Vichyssoise (10 oz. each)
1 tablespoon curry powder
2 teaspoons powdered ginger
1 cup cold milk
salt
pepper

Place the Vichyssoise in a bowl. In a smaller bowl, put the curry powder and ginger. Pour in the chilled milk and stir until the curry and ginger are dissolved. Add to the Vichyssoise and stir well. Correct seasoning if necessary and serve at once.

II. Soup Senegalese (*Traditional Version*)

(*Serves* 4)

1 large onion
2 large stalks celery
1 medium apple
1 large chicken breast, cooked
1½ tablespoons butter
1½ tablespoons sifted flour
1 tablespoon curry powder
2 teaspoons powdered ginger
3 pints rich chicken stock
1 bay leaf
¾ cup light cream
salt
pepper

Chop the onion and the celery coarsely. Peel and dice the apple. Cut the chicken into fine dice, not larger than a quarter of an inch. Melt the butter in a saucepan, and cook the onion and celery until both are soft, but do not allow to brown. Add flour, curry powder, and ginger, and make a roux (G). When roux is ready, transfer contents of the saucepan to a blender. Add the apple, half the chicken—keep the other half in a cold place—and one cup of chicken stock. Blend for thirty seconds at high speed. Return to saucepan, add remaining chicken broth and bay leaf. Bring to a boil, and simmer for five minutes. Remove and discard bay leaf. Transfer soup to a bowl and place in refrigerator until needed. (The soup will gain from an overnight stay in the cold.) Just before serving, stir in the chilled cream, taste, and add salt and pepper as required. Garnish with reserved chicken dice and serve forthwith.

SUGGESTED MENU

Most midsummer meals should have, I think, at least one hot item in addition to coffee. In this instance I would serve hot corn sticks. The soup could well be followed by almost any salad. There is a very good, light dry white wine from Austria called Ginsinger. Try it with this soup.

JADE SOUP MARY DULANY HUNTER

(Serves 4)

Jade here refers to the color of the soup, not to: the verb, the mineral, the woman, or the river. The recipe comes in a rather round-about way from Aix-en-Provence to Cairo, to Maine, to California, to Washington, to Vernal, Utah, and back to Washington.

In some respects, perhaps, it should be called "Lucky Strike Soup" because a package of "Luckies" was instrumental in obtaining the recipe.

The first recorded version of this soup was served at Aix-en-Provence to an American couple posted to the United States Embassy in Cairo. The waiter at the French inn was young and efficient. He had served on a Free French destroyer during World War II and had put in at both New York and Norfolk. When he discovered how much the Americans liked the soup and noticed a package of Luckies on the table he became even more efficient and most solicitous. He offered to get Madame the recipe.

Procuring a recipe from a French, Italian, or Spanish chef is not dissimilar to climbing Everest or scuba-diving to four hundred feet. It can be done, but the effort is stupendous. In the case of Everest and recipes, money helps. But in this instance the obvious enjoyment of the soup by the diners and the sight of the American cigarettes—one suspects they ended in the waiter's pocket—were sufficient. The couple got the recipe.

In Cairo, Achmed, the Embassy cook, added a dash of spice. The revised version was brought back through Maine to Washington, where it eventually underwent another change or two, suggested by several people with a fine taste in food. Thence it, the recipe, traveled with Mary Hunter to Entrance Wilderness in Utah, whence came permission to share the soup, in another slightly altered form, with the gentle reader, whoever he may be. Nothing has been lost by its various metamorphoses. It is a splendid luncheon or supper dish.

In its traditional version the making of Jade Soup is a long and somewhat tedious process. The first step is the preparation of the watercress, which alone takes longer than all of Version I.

When Jade Soup arrived once more in Washington, the recipe had been stabilized for some time and the soup was prepared as in II.

I. Jade Soup Mary Dulany Hunter (*Quick Version*)

(*Serves 4*)

2 heads Boston lettuce
3 tablespoons butter
bouquet garni (G)
 (½ teaspoon basil
 ½ teaspoon thyme
 ½ teaspoon marjoram)
4 cans Cream of Watercress Soup (10 oz. each)
1¼ cups milk
4 tablespoons cognac

Remove and discard the tough outer leaves and the cores of the lettuce. Wash leaves, dry, and chop coarsely. Melt butter in a large saucepan, put in the chopped lettuce and cook over a moderate fire, stirring frequently to coat the leaves with butter. Cook until the lettuce is about to turn brown. When lettuce is done, after approximately twenty minutes, remove and drain on paper towels. While it is cooling, place the Watercress Soup in the saucepan. Add bouquet garni, milk, and cognac. Cook very slowly over a gentle flame for twenty minutes. Keep the contents of the pan just under a simmer, and on no account allow it to boil. While soup is cooking, mince the lettuce very fine indeed, and add to the soup. Stir well. Remove bouquet garni, and correct seasoning. It may require a little pepper. If soup is too thick for your taste, thin to the desired consistency with a little milk, heat through, and serve at once.

II. Jade Soup Mary Dulany Hunter (*Traditional Version*)

(*Serves 4*)

2 bunches watercress
2 heads Boston lettuce
6 tablespoons butter
5 pints beef stock
bouquet garni (G)
 (½ teaspoon basil
 ½ teaspoon thyme
 ½ teaspoon marjoram)
¾ teaspoon salt
¼ teaspoon freshly ground pepper
4 egg yolks
1 cup light cream
1 cup heavy cream
2 tablespoons sifted flour
4 tablespoons good cognac

Remove the leaves from each sprig of watercress, reserving four sprigs; discard the stems. This little chore, if you have fast hands, will take about an hour. Chop the watercress well and set aside. Remove and discard the coarse outer leaves and the core of the lettuce. Chop lettuce coarsely. Put four tablespoons butter in the top of a large double boiler, at least three-quart capacity, and melt over direct heat. Put in the chopped watercress and lettuce, and cook over a moderate flame, stirring frequently to coat all the greens with butter, for about eight minutes, or until all juice from greens has disappeared and they are about to turn brown. The odor may seem unpleasant, but persevere. Add the stock, the bouquet garni, the salt, and pepper. Bring to a boil, and simmer for one hour. Discard bouquet garni and allow contents of pot to cool for about half an hour. Put through a blender at moderate speed for fifteen seconds. Return to pot and warm slightly. Meanwhile, place egg yolks in a bowl, add both creams, and beat with a wire whisk until well blended. Slowly add about three tablespoons of the warm soup to the bowl, stir well, and then gradually add contents of bowl to the soup, stirring constantly. In another saucepan place remaining butter, melt, and add flour to make a roux (G). When the roux is cooked, gradually add two cups of the warm soup, beating the while over a low flame, to make a sauce. When sauce is cooked—when it has come to a boil—add it to the soup, stirring it in well. Place soup in double boiler over hot water and heat over a high flame until it is just ready to simmer. Never, but never, let it boil once the cream has been added. Stir in Cognac. Garnish with reserved sprigs of watercress, and serve.

SUGGESTED MENU

Vienna rolls are most appropriate with Jade Soup. Eschew lettuce in the salad and serve cold artichokes with Vinaigrette Dressing (G). A Rhine wine or a Mosel complements the soup very well.

GLOSSARY

Cooking Terms
and Some Non-Soup Recipes
Mentioned in This Book
Together with
An APPENDIX of
Soup Kitchen
Utensils

BÉCHAMEL SAUCE. One of the most important sauces in any cookbook is Béchamel. There are two methods of making it, a quick version and a traditional one. The latter is, I think, by far the better but requires more time. Both versions follow as I and II.

I. Béchamel Sauce (*Quick Version*)

(*About 3 Cups*)

1 small onion
4½ tablespoons butter
4½ tablespoons sifted flour
4 cups milk
salt
pepper

Mince onion and set aside. Melt butter in a saucepan over direct but low heat. Put in onion and cook slowly for five minutes, stirring frequently to keep onion from browning. Add the flour and make a roux (G). When roux has cooked about five minutes, remove pan from fire. Pour milk into another saucepan and gradually bring to a simmer. Return roux to a low fire, and gradually add hot milk, stirring constantly with a wooden spoon until mixture is smooth and has come to a simmer again. Allow to simmer one minute. Taste, correct seasoning as needed with salt and pepper. Drain through a chinoise (p. 194), working the wooden spoon around the sides of the chinoise until all the sauce has gone through. It is now ready for use

II. Béchamel Sauce (*Traditional Version*)

(*About 3 Cups*)

¼ pound lean veal
1 small onion
5½ tablespoons butter
4½ tablespoons sifted flour
4 cups milk
½ teaspoon thyme
1 teaspoon freshly ground white pepper
½ teaspoon freshly ground nutmeg

Chop the veal into half-inch cubes, mince the onion very fine, and set both aside. Melt four and a half tablespoons butter in the top of a double boiler over direct but low heat. Put in onion and cook slowly for five minutes. Stir frequently to prevent browning.

Add flour to make a roux (G), stirring again to avoid burning. When roux has cooked five minutes, remove from fire. Pour the milk into a saucepan and bring gradually to a simmer. While the milk is heating, place the remaining butter in a small skillet, melt, and add the veal, thyme, pepper, and nutmeg. Cook for five minutes, stirring of course. Just before milk simmers return roux to fire and heat. As soon as milk simmers, remove hot roux from fire and pour milk on it. Stir with a wire whisk. Keep stirring until sauce comes to a boil. Boil one minute. Place the sauce over hot water, stir in contents of skillet, and continue to cook over hot water for one hour. Stir sauce every fifteen minutes. Strain sauce through a chinoise, as in 1, and it is ready for use. If it is not required immediately dot the surface with small dabs of butter, which will melt to form an airtight seal and prevent formation of a skin.

BLANCH. To blanch is to parboil, usually in lightly salted water, some meats, or some vegetables, for a very short time so as to soften them, or occasionally to alter the taste. In most instances blanching should take less than five minutes.

BOMBAY DUCK. Despite its name this is a fish and not one of our feathered friends. In India a species of lizard fish is cleaned, cut open, and seasoned with herbs and salt and allowed to dry in the sun. When completely dry it is shredded and used as a condiment, particularly with curries. Do not judge the taste by the smell.

BOUQUET GARNI. Bouquet garnis are used extensively, especially in French recipes, to give the flavor of herbs and spices to dishes, without mixing them with the other ingredients. A bouquet garni is made by placing the appropriate herbs and spices on a square of cheesecloth and tying the corners together to make a small bag. The cloth allows the flavors to come through but holds the flavoring agents themselves inside. Before the dish is served the bouquet garni is removed. Where a bouquet garni is required in any of the soup recipes its ingredients are specified.

BRIGID'S BREAD. This recipe makes a fine example of that quick soda bread which is so well made and so much esteemed in Eire. I haven't the remotest idea who the original Brigid was but my instructor in baking was not named Brigid.

BRIGID'S BREAD

(*Serves 4–6*)

4 cups presifted flour
2 teaspoons baking powder
3 teaspoons sugar
2 teaspoons salt
4 tablespoons lard
1 tablespoon caraway seed
1 cup buttermilk

Place the flour, baking powder, sugar, and salt in a bowl. Mix well. Sift the contents of the bowl into another one until they have been put through the sifter three times. Cut in the lard. Stir the caraway seed into the mixture. Make a well in the center and gradually add the buttermilk. Slowly mix flour mixture in from the outside toward the center, adding buttermilk as you work. Sometimes you will wish for a third hand. When the liquid is well mixed in the dough should be somewhat moist. Transfer it to a floured bread board and knead lightly for about five minutes. Divide the dough into twelve equal parts, and shape each into a mound. Cut a large X in the top of each, and bake in a preheated hot oven (450 degrees) for forty-five minutes. It should be served immediately as the crust has a tendency to harden if kept waiting.

CELESTIAL SALAD. Although the Chinese are not great salad eaters, this book contains a number of soups from the Celestial Kingdom. But for those who might like a salad with their soup, regardless of its origin, this salad was devised. It is strictly ersatz Chinese, but is a good accompaniment to any soup in which none of the salad ingredients appears.

CELESTIAL SALAD

(*Serves 6*)

1 small Chinese cabbage
1 cup canned water chestnuts
1 cup canned bean sprouts
½ cup raw snow peas
1 teaspoon dry mustard
2 teaspoons soy sauce
½ cup French dressing (G)

Shred the tender leaves of the cabbage to make two cups and place in a salad bowl. Drain the water chestnuts and the bean sprouts. Slice the water chestnuts thin, and cut snow peas into thirds. Add all three to the salad bowl. Add soy sauce and mustard to the French dressing, stir until mustard is dissolved, and pour over the salad.

CROUTONS. Croutons come, as do girls, in a variety of sizes and shapes, all of them useful and many very zesty. Some are more difficult to make than others, but none are too difficult. For the purposes of this book, I have divided them, the croutons, into three classes: two large and one small. The large ones are intended for use in such soups as French Onion and Vegetable. Small croutons are employed in many of the thick smooth soups: the bisques and the cream soups. Large croutons are single pieces of bread intended to give body to what are basically thin soups, while small croutons act as a kind of garnish to give "crunchiness" to thick soups.

The simplest way and probably the best way to make large croutons is to let some of your leftover French bread get stale. Whenever I have French bread, I allow the uneaten pieces to stay out in the air for a few hours to dry out and then keep them in a plastic bag in the refrigerator until needed. They should be browned in the oven just before use.

Another variety of large crouton, although there is some argument about whether these should be called croutons or fried bread—it is a matter of semantics—is made as follows:

Four Croutons

4 slices white bread | **3 tablespoons butter**

Remove crust from bread. Using a thin glass or a round cookie cutter, of a diameter a little less than the width of the bread, cut rounds from each slice. Place the butter in a skillet, brown the butter and put in the bread rounds. Cook slowly, turning from time to time, until the bread is brown on both sides. Drain on brown paper or kitchen towels. You now have four large croutons.

My friend to whom this book is dedicated insists with some vehemence that these are not croutons but garnish, and backs up her argument with logical reasoning and quotations from various authoritative cookbooks. Regardless of who is right, these "croutons" can well substitute for those first mentioned, if no French bread is available.

While small croutons are easy to make, you may substitute a commercial product known as "Croutettes" made by Kellogg. They are intended as stuffing for various kinds of fowl, and are seasoned with herbs. They do very well in most soups. Normally small croutons are prepared in the following manner. For four servings of soup use:

Small Croutons

3 slices bread
½ cup shortening (bacon fat, cooking oil, Crisco)

Remove the crusts from the bread. Cut the bread into half-inch cubes. Place the fat in a small skillet, heat over a moderate flame until very hot. Put in the bread cubes, and, using a slotted spoon, keep turning the cubes in the hot fat until each is well browned on all sides. Drain the cubes on paper towels or brown paper. They are now ready to serve.

Large croutons are placed in the soup plate and the soup is poured over them. Small croutons are either served in a saucer or bowl beside each diner, so that he may use as many as he desires and as he desires them, or are placed in the soup just before it is served, whether in a tureen or on individual plates. Again, as with girls, it all depends on the circumstances.

FILÉ GUMBO. This powder is a combination of dried sassafras leaves, dried okra, and several spices, depending upon who makes it. The ingredients are mixed and powdered very fine either in a mortar or by machinery. The concoction is believed to have been invented by the Choctaw Indians living in the bayou country. It was alleged to have some curative powers. In any case, it is now extensively used in the same area, in and around New Orleans, in the thickening of soups and sauces. One word of caution: once it is added to a recipe, the dish must not be allowed to boil, or the filé gumbo will become stringy and impart a bitter taste. It is marketed widely. It is sometimes marketed as gumbo filé.

FISH SHOYU SAUCE. This is an oriental sauce made especially for use with fish or seafood dishes and differs considerably from ordinary shoyu sauce. It can be purchased in most oriental grocery stores. One version, made in Hong Kong by Lee Seng Heng, is called "Fish's Gravy." Other varieties are, no doubt, just as good. Its use with oriental fish or seafood soups improves the taste more than regular shoyu or soy sauce.

FRENCH DRESSING. French dressing is probably the most important of all thin salad dressings because on it are based a wide variety of others. It is also the simplest of all dressings to make, as it requires but four ingredients.

French Dressing
(1 Cup)

¾ cup olive oil
¼ cup wine vinegar
½ teaspoon salt
¼ teaspoon freshly ground pepper

Place the first three ingredients in a bowl. Grind the pepper into them. Stir well with a fork, and you have French dressing. It will mix a little better if the bowl is placed in a larger one containing cracked ice, but this refinement is not essential. The dressing, stored in a glass-stoppered bottle, will keep almost indefinitely; never put it in the refrigerator.

Regardless of commercial "French" dressings, or those served at restaurants, a real French dressing can contain only those ingredients, no more no less. Adding others may and frequently does make an excellent salad dressing but it is not French.

HARD FLOUR. Used mostly in making such pasta as macaroni, spaghetti, ravioli, and other products usually associated with Italy. Hard flour is milled the same way as ordinary flour, but is made from hard wheat, and contains a higher gluten content than ordinary flour. It may be purchased under the name of Hard Flour in some good grocery stores or Italian markets.

HAZEL'S HERBAGE. My friend Hazel, who is more than a good cook—she is an imaginative one—invented this salad because her husband was adamant in his refusal to eat hothouse tomatoes—who can blame him? Hazel's invention is the only nondessert salad in which, to my mind, fresh fruit is acceptable.

HAZEL'S HERBAGE
(Serves 4)

16 leaves Boston lettuce
2 navel oranges
2 small onions
4 ounces ripe blue cheese
French dressing (G)

Wash lettuce leaves, dry between towels, and place in refrigerator to crisp. Peel oranges, removing all white pulp. Slice oranges as thin as possible. Peel onions and slice them as thin as possible. Separate slices into rings. Place lettuce leaves in a salad bowl.

Make a layer of orange slices, and with studied abandon arrange onion rings over the oranges. Crumble the cheese and spread it over the salad. Cover with French dressing, toss well, and serve.

HOFBURG SALAD. Before World War I and the subsequent dissolution of the Austro-Hungarian Empire, the Hofburg was the palace of the emperor. No one can be certain that this specific salad was served at the Hofburg, but similar ones undoubtedly were.

HOFBURG SALAD

(*Serves 4*)

(The dressing is an integral part of the recipe and is made along with the salad itself)

16 leaves Bibb lettuce
1 small celery root
1 thin cucumber
1 medium tomato
½ cup mayonnaise
½ cup sour cream
1 teaspoon olive oil
1 teaspoon freshly ground black pepper
2 teaspoons minced chives

Wash lettuce. Wrap in towels and place in refrigerator to dry and crisp. Scrape celery root, and chop into quarter-inch dice. Place in salad bowl. Score cucumber lengthwise with a silver fork, remove and discard one end about an inch long. With a very sharp knife cut twenty-four very thin slices and add them to the bowl. Skin tomato, and chop into half-inch cubes. Add cubes to the bowl. In another and smaller bowl, place the mayonnaise, sour cream, olive oil, and pepper. Mix thoroughly. Reserve three tablespoons, and pour remainder over vegetables in bowl. Mix slowly until all ingredients are coated. Arrange lettuce leaves on four salad plates. On each bed of lettuce, arrange six of the cucumber slices. Mix the celery root and tomato well and divide the mixture among the four plates, forming mounds. On each mound put a smaller mound of the reserved dressing. Garnish each with finely chopped chives. Serve chilled.

KING COLE SLAW. Seated one day in the King Cole Bar in New York City and admiring Maxfield Parrish's famous mural which gives the bar its name, I apparently had too many martinis. I had been contemplating a new kind of slaw. After a time I looked more closely at the mural and it seemed to me that one of the fiddlers had a green head, another red hair, and the third was obviously Chinese. I weaved my way back to my hotel. I had not only the recipe for the new slaw but a name for it as well.

KING COLE SLAW

(*Serves 4*)

½ small head green cabbage
½ small head red cabbage
1 small head Chinese cabbage, leafy end only
½ cup mayonnaise
2 tablespoons dill seed
salt
fresh pepper

Shred the three cabbages and place in a salad bowl. In a smaller bowl put the mayonnaise and dill seed. Mix thoroughly. Add contents of small bowl to the cabbages and stir with a wooden fork and spoon until all leaves are well coated. Taste and add salt and pepper as required. Stir again and serve cold.

MARYLAND BEATEN BISCUIT. Two things are essential in the preparation of this delectable bread: a Boy Scout ax and a strong right—or left—arm. Sinister biscuits are preferred by some to the dexter variety. If you have a Boy Scout handy, his good deed for the day would be beating the dough. It is possible to use an ice mallet for this chore, or a double-bitted ax. But the former requires real pounding; a full-sized ax is a little heavy for most cooks outside of lumber camps. The weight of a Scout ax is enough to do the work if it is allowed to fall on the dough.

Beaten biscuits have many uses besides accompanying soups. One use is to split them, lightly butter each cut side, insert a goodly quantity of Smithfield ham to make spherical sandwiches, and serve them with cocktails, or merely for lunch. In either case make an appreciable number. This recipe yields about twenty-four biscuits.

MARYLAND BEATEN BISCUIT

4 cups flour
1 teaspoon salt
1 tablespoon sugar
1 teaspoon baking powder
¼ cup chilled lard
½ cup cold milk
½ cup ice water
3 tablespoons butter

It should be noted that in rainy or humid weather the quantity of liquid should be reduced slightly. Place the first four ingredients together in a bowl. Place them in a sifter and sift three times (once only if you possess a triple sifter). Using a knife or a pastry blender, cut the lard into the dry mixture until it assumes the consistency of water-ground cornmeal. Mix milk and ice water. Add to mixture and mix to make a stiff dough. Place the dough on a strong support, and start beating with the Boy Scout ax. The dough should be folded frequently. It makes the dough better and gives a little relief to the arm. The beating and folding process should, nay must, continue for at least half an hour—in this case forty whacks or even forty-one are totally insufficient. When the dough has been beaten enough, let your arm relax for a brief time and beat the dough five minutes more. The dough should be smooth, elastic, and well blistered. Roll the dough on a floured board to a thickness of one-half inch and cut it into one-and-a-half-inch rounds. By rubbing between the palms, form the dough into spheres. Grease a cookie sheet lightly with butter. Melt the remaining butter. Place biscuits on the sheet. Stab each lightly on top with a sharp three-tined fork. Brush lightly with butter, and bake for forty minutes in a preheated medium oven (325 degrees). Serve very hot. The biscuits should not be allowed to stand once they have been shaped but put into the oven as rapidly as possible.

MUSTARD DRESSING. This is French dressing with mustard added and a very good dressing it is if the salad be particularly bland.

Mustard Dressing
(*About 1 Cup*)

¼ cup wine vinegar
2 teaspoons dry mustard
¾ cup olive oil
½ teaspoon salt
¼ teaspoon freshly ground pepper

Place vinegar in a small bowl, add dry mustard and stir with a teaspoon or fork until the mustard has dissolved. Place the other ingredients in a larger bowl. When ready to serve add the contents of the smaller bowl to the larger, put in an ice cube and stir very hard until the dressing has melded. Discard the ice and serve the dressing.

OLD MAN SEAN'S SALLET. According to Irish legend, Old Man Sean lived in a shanty on the bank of the Liffey, hard by Dublin. He is said to have obtained the recipe for his sallet from the Shee. "Sallet," incidentally, is Gaelic for salad. But wherever he got the recipe, or indeed whether he existed at all except in the legend, is unimportant, because the salad has much to recommend it and is ideal with or after certain soups.

OLD MAN SEAN'S SALLET

(*Serves 4*)

1 clove garlic
1 medium carrot
1 medium turnip
8 sprigs watercress
4 small sprigs field cress
3 small leeks
12 small crisp lettuce leaves
French dressing (G)

Peel the garlic, cut it in half, and rub the inside of a salad bowl well with the cut side of each half. Scrape the carrot and peel the turnip, and cut each into medium dice. Chop the two cresses very coarsely. Remove and discard the green tops from the leeks. Chop the white parts into half-inch slices. Place all the vegetables in the salad bowl, pour over them about a quarter of a cup of French dressing. Mix well. Place three lettuce leaves on each of four salad plates. Spread the contents of the salad bowl over the lettuce leaves and serve well chilled.

PONTALBA SALAD. This is an old Southern dish, named after the Pontalba Mansions in New Orleans. The buildings are well over a hundred years old and reputed to be the oldest apartment houses in the United States. There is, however, nothing ancient about the salad. It is rich and delicious.

PONTALBA SALAD

(*Serves 2*)

4 slices lean bacon
2 medium scallions
2 large pimentos
1 medium avocado
1 tablespoon fresh lemon juice
1 tablespoon Worcestershire sauce
2 tablespoons olive oil
½ teaspoon freshly ground black pepper
½ teaspoon salt
4 large lettuce leaves

Place bacon in a skillet and cook slowly until done. Remove to paper towels to drain and become crisp. While bacon is cooking, mince the scallions, including most of the green tops, and dice the pimentos. Slice the avocado in half lengthwise. Remove and discard the seed. Scoop out the meat with a spoon, keeping the shells intact, and place it in a mixing bowl. By now the bacon should be crisp and cool. Crumble it. Add the bacon and all other ingredients except lettuce to the bowl and mix thoroughly with a fork, being sure that the avocado meat is mashed well. Taste and correct the seasoning with additional salt or pepper if needed. Stuff half the mixture into each avocado half. Arrange two lettuce leaves on each of two salad plates, and place the stuffed avocado halves on them. Keep refrigerated until the salad is served.

SALADE FLANDRE. Flanders is famous for many things both historical and culinary. One of the latter is Belgian endive—the English call it chicory. Endive is delicious as a salad ingredient.

SALADE FLANDRE

(*Serves 4*)

4 large stalks Belgian endive
1 medium leek
8 Brussels sprouts
12 cherry tomatoes

Chop off and discard the base of each stalk of endive. Cut each stalk in half. Separate the leaves and place them in a salad bowl. Wash leek thoroughly and cut off the top about two inches above the white. Discard the top and slice the remainder into rounds about an eighth of an inch thick. Spread over the endive. Remove bottoms and outer leaves of sprouts and discard. Cut each sprout in half vertically and add to the salad. Wash the tomatoes, cut them in half, and arrange, cut side up, on the salad. Toss with French dressing or with mayonnaise, depending on the soup. With a clear soup, mayonnaise is the obvious choice.

RUSSIAN DRESSING. This splendid dressing is named Russian because it contains caviar, although the best caviar comes from the Caspian Sea and is as much Iranian as Russian. You should include this dressing in your culinary repertoire.

Russian Dressing

(About 1¾ cups)

1 cup mayonnaise
3 tablespoons lumpfish caviar
¼ cup chili sauce or catsup
1 teaspoon grated onion

Combine above ingredients and chill until ready to serve.

ROUX. Roux is a combination of shortening, usually butter, and flour, cooked together. Its purpose is to thicken or give body to sauces. The quantity of the roux will determine the quantity of the sauce and its thickness. Normally a roux is made of equal amounts of butter and flour, i.e., one tablespoon of butter to one of flour. Melt the butter in a saucepan, and over a low flame, gradually add in the flour, stirring with a wooden spoon. Continue cooking and stirring until the roux is cooked to a pale golden brown, a matter of four to mix minutes depending on the quantity. If a brown roux is required, cook until colored light brown. In each of the foregoing soup recipes where a roux is required the proportions of butter to flour are given.

SCOTCH BONNET. A sauce for flavoring soups and sauces, Scotch Bonnet is one of the hottest peppers known. It grows, of course, in Scotland but is rare in the United States. Among other places it grows in the vicinity of Philadelphia. Near there, at Ivyland, Pennsylvania, the firm of John Wagner and Sons combines it with sherry to make a condiment which, so far as I know, is unique. It is marketed in very attractive ounce-and-a-half bottles under the name of "Borie's Scotch Bonnet." It is difficult to find except in well-stocked grocery stores or specialty shops. It is worth the search.

VELOUTÉ SAUCE. Velouté means velvet, and, properly made, Velouté sauce tastes the way velvet feels: smooth. It is made almost the same way as Béchamel, except that instead of milk you use beef stock, chicken stock, or fish stock (see Section I for basic stocks). The kind of stock will be determined by the kind of soup you wish to thicken.

Velouté Sauce

(About 4 Cups)

4 tablespoons butter
6 tablespoons sifted flour
4 cups stock
1 teaspoon salt
1 teaspoon fresh pepper

Place the butter in a two-quart saucepan. When it has melted over a low fire, add the flour and mix well with a wooden spoon to make a roux (G). Stir constantly to prevent burning and continue to cook for about five minutes. While making the roux, bring the stock almost to a boil in another saucepan. When roux is done, remove from fire and pour in the boiling stock, stirring the while with a wire whisk. Return to fire and continue stirring until the mixture has come to a boil. Allow to boil one minute. *Et voici la sauce velouté.*

VINAIGRETTE DRESSING. Vinaigrette is another variation on French dressing and is a splendid seasoning for cold artichokes, asparagus salad, or even some of the mixed green salads.

Vinaigrette Dressing

(*About 1 Cup*)

- ¾ cup olive oil
- ½ cup tarragon vinegar
- 1 scant teaspoon dry mustard
- 1½ teaspoons minced parsley
- 1 teaspoon very finely minced scallion
- ½ teaspoon salt
- ¼ teaspoon white pepper

This dressing is best mixed over cracked ice. (Failing that, use a pint bowl and add an ice cube while mixing.) Place oil, vinegar, and mustard in the bowl and beat frantically with a fork until all the mustard has been dissolved. Add the remaining ingredients, stir well, and serve. If the dressing is not needed at once, do not refrigerate; place in a tightly covered jar. It will keep for almost a week except in the very hottest weather. Stir well just before use. If serving with cold artichokes, pour a generous portion of the dressing over each artichoke.

APPENDIX

(While you may be able to make do without all of the items listed here, you will find that their possession will lessen your labors in making soups.)

BLENDER. Almost all modern kitchens boast a blender. If yours does not you can still make all the soups in this book but your work will be infinitely more difficult and time-consuming. A blender with several speeds is desirable.

CHINOISE. This is a kind of kitchen strainer, conical in shape and approximately seven inches in diameter at the top and seven inches long. It is much stronger than the normal kitchen strainer and has two layers of very fine mesh. It is extremely useful for straining soups, sauces, and gravies and will save you many hours of work in eliminating lumps in sauces or soups.

MOULI GRATER. One of the greatest kitchen inventions since the skillet, this hand-operated mechanical gadget will grate cheese, nuts, and almost any other food which has to be either chopped or grated. It is definitely superior to the normal flat type of kitchen grater. The grating is done by a cylinder. Three types of cylinders are available for small, medium, and large grating. The Mouli grater is a great time and effort saver.

PASTA MACHINE. Except for those who want to make their own noodles, this equipment is unnecessary. Its use requires a great deal of space and many paper towels. Once the dough has been thinned by running it through the machine and the noodles have been cut to proper size, they should be spread out at full length on paper towels and allowed to dry. Once dried, they can be kept almost indefinitely until you are ready to boil and use them. Like the old-fashioned manually operated meat grinder, the pasta machine attaches to a table with a clamp. The table should be at least three feet long. While the space necessary for drying the noodles will depend on the quantity, you should have a counter at least six feet long and about eighteen inches wide for the drying process.

SAUCEPANS AND DOUBLE BOILERS. You will need at least two double boilers with lids. One of the utensils, preferably both, should have a capacity of three quarts, although one of three quarts and one of two quarts will suffice. The lower pans of the double boilers will, of course, frequently be required as saucepans. Presumably you will already have at least two saucepans—one quart and two quarts, and at least one skillet ten inches in diameter.

SKIMMER. This is a most useful implement for removing scum which rises to the surface while certain soups are cooking. It is almost essential for taking heavy grease off the top of cold stock. The implement resembles a flat ladle approximately four and a half inches in diameter with holes in the bottom. It has a long handle which is set at almost a right angle to the bowl. This implement is useless for removing fat or grease from the top of a warm stock or soup. The best method for removing this grease is to drop paper towels gently onto the surface, and slowly slide across and discard. It may take several applications of paper towels but it is the easiest way to remove unwanted fat from the surface of any hot liquid.

SOUP KETTLE. Probably the most important implement for making soup is a heavy iron soup kettle with a capacity of between six and seven quarts. In my opinion the best of these kettles is made by Creusot. It should, of course, have a lid.

SOUP PLATES. Soup plates or bowls are not exactly kitchen utensils, but when one is serving hearty soups a note will be helpful. Normal bouillon cups or cream soups are too small for serving the dishes described in this book. A bouillon cup holds only about four ounces; a cream soup, about eight. What you will require are soup plates or large soup bowls which hold at least fifteen ounces, preferably a pint. In one way bowls are better, as the surface exposed to the air is smaller and the soup stays hot longer. Tepid soup is a curse.

WIRE WHISKS. A wire whisk is essential for breaking up lumps in soups or sauces. I believe that, while not essential, two of these are helpful. One should be twelve inches long and the other eight.

WOODEN SPOONS. Two long-handled wooden spoons are required for making roux (G) and stirring sauces.

INDEX